Running for Neil

My journey to complete the London Marathon

John Adam

ISBN-10: 1499167636:
ISBN-13: 978-1499167634

DEDICATION

This book is written in memory of my brother Neil Adam who sadly passed away on the 21st January 2012 from Cancer. He displayed an amazing spirit throughout his illness which he fought with absolute dignity.

CONTENTS

ACKNOWLEDGMENTS

This book would never have been possible without the support of many people, but in particular my lovely wife Annalise who has been by my side every step of this journey and for that I thank her.

Friends and colleagues have also been incredibly supportive as well as generous; their words of encouragement have really helped me over the last eighteen months.

Last, but definitely not least, the Real Buzz community of fellow runners who I have come to know so well, your support and advice has been invaluable without which I would never have made it to the start line let alone finished.

PROLOGUE

On 21 January 2012 my brother lost his fight against cancer and passed away peacefully on a Sunday evening with his family around him. He had a rare spinal cancer, only 10 cases diagnosed in the world today. Given less than a year to live he set about raising money for Cancer Research UK and despite the very aggressive nature of the cancer he had a determination to live that gave him almost six months more than the original prognosis. Sadly, he never got to see the spring of 2012, something he was looking forward to.

The day he died I decided to carry on his fund-raising activities and determined to run the London Marathon in his memory. This is the story of what turned out to be one of the biggest challenges of my life and one which has an added element I did not expect. In keeping an online diary of my training I became part of the Real Buzz community and there is no doubt that I would never have made it to the start line if it were not for the support and encouragement I received during my training and for that I am extremely grateful. These wonderful and sometimes crazy individuals all know who they are, their words of wisdom have kept me going and I thank them all for their inspirational advice.

During the last two years I never ever lost sight of why I had challenged myself in this way and Neil was always in my thoughts, on every run I ever did. For that reason I thought it useful to highlight a selection of the conversations we had through email. As the cancer began to affect him more and more it reveals the sort of man he was and the brother I lost.

Dear John
I'm sorry, no news from me for a long time and now I'm afraid it's bad news. Thought I should let you know, I suffered back and leg pains over the last couple of weeks. I had an MRI scan yesterday and have been diagnosed with a tumour in my spinal cord. It's a great shock to us. I will be admitted to hospital this evening and operated on tomorrow.

Neil sent me another email later saying "don't worry bruv, I'll get through this"

Neil and I had spoken briefly on the phone, but he emailed the next day to confirm that he had a tumour in his spine and would be having an operation. As he was living and working in Turkey at the time this was a little bit of a concern, but he had private health insurance through his company and so he was in good hands.

Obviously this came as a huge shock to us all, but Neil assured me that it was just routine and it would most likely turn out to be benign. That was Neil, always positive in his outlook, but I knew that this was much more serious and Neil knew it as well. There was nothing we could do however save wait for the operation and hope for the best possible outcome.

1 EARLY LIFE

Neil was one of a kind and there is not a day goes by that I don't think of him. We were different in many ways, but we also had many things in common, none more so than a daft sense of humour and a liking for the absurdities of life. Given our family history, more of which later, we were never a 'normal' family, but despite this we had an idyllic childhood, mostly due to the real rock of the family, our mother. Being much younger than Neil I obviously idolised him from a very young age and he in turn looked after me. Strangely, despite the odd brotherly squabbles, we never argued or fell out once, although I am sure my brother was exasperated by my behaviour from time to time.

He was six years older than me, the first born son and I was the fifth, but we were the only two children my mother and father had. My mother miscarried three times between my brother and I due to complications related to blood type. It is not a problem nowadays, but rhesus negative babies were quite an issue in the fifties, so I was a much wanted child, born prematurely and had a blood transfusion immediately I came into the world.

Neil used to tell me that every time our mother miscarried he got a train set, funny what you remember when you are a child, although he noticed the sadness in the house. To lose three children must have been awful and something I can't imagine, but my mother never really talked about it, she came from an era that just got on with things. Being a child during the Second World War she witnessed unbelievable destruction and mayhem and seemed to have a very relaxed attitude to life.

The world was a very different place in the fifties and our father ruled the house, his word was law and it was not a good idea to upset him. Knowing what I know now I can see why he was the way he was as he had had a tough life as a child. His father was a doctor in the Indian Army in the days when settlers from abroad were encouraged to marry native women and so dad was an Anglo-Indian, but he lived a reasonably privileged life. He was raised by servants until packed off to school miles away from home though he hated his days there, being a Catholic boarding school the teachers would punish him severely for any little thing.

I remember him telling me how he had to hold his hand out for punishments and the ruler they used had holes in which would raise welts on his palm. Not surprisingly dad was a bit of a rebel and despite being quite slight he stood up to the obligatory boarding school bullies so that no one messed with 'Mad Adam' as he became known. He had a quick temper, but he wasn't stupid which made him quite an adversary and clearly our father was not one to cross.

Life changed dramatically for him when his father was killed in Burma during the war by which time he had already joined the Merchant Navy and sailed around the World. However partition in India resulted in the rest of his family coming over to England and, for reasons known only to him, he jumped ship in New Zealand and made his way to the UK. Arriving on the south coast he travelled to London and eventually met my mother at India House on the Strand where she worked. Mum happened to be engaged to someone else at the time, but soon broke it off after having her head turned by dad as, despite everything, he was quite a charmer when he wanted to be.

Whereas dad was from a large family with three sisters and one brother, mum was an only child. She had a poor relationship with her mother, she could never do anything right in her eyes, but she was the apple of her father's eye who she idolised. Although I respected dad for what he achieved in his life, it was mum who made my childhood what it was. Totally unflappable, she lived by the mantra 'what will be will be' as nothing ever bothered her. She hated a fuss and she never made one and though I am sure she must have been devastated by the loss of not just one, but three babies, I never once heard her complain about her lot in life, she just got on with things.

I guess they complemented each other, my father had a terrible temper, but my mother was as calm as you could be and though I am not convinced they had the best of marriages, there is no doubt that they loved each other. Neil was very much like dad though and was very driven in what he did, dad worked very hard to achieve what he did in life and Neil was the same, unfortunately being so similar they often clashed at home and they had a very poor relationship. Nothing my brother ever did was good enough for our father, though I am sure, being a parent myself, that this was borne out of wanting the best for his first born son.

I obviously know very little of what Neil was like when he was quite young other than he tested my parents to the full. To say he was a bit of a maverick would be an understatement; he lived life to the full often to the detriment of those closest to him. If Neil wanted to do something, then he did it regardless of the consequences. When he was very young he would cycle his tricycle at top speed towards the wall and then jump off at the last minute to watch it crash. I have no idea what my parents would thought of such behaviour, though I suspect they were still wondering how to deal with the fact that he had previously 'oiled' the wheels with sand! Neil

6

needed challenges, he always had a plan and was constantly coming up with ideas for various projects, again regardless of the effect his antics might have on those around him.

One well told story of his early years could not highlight this any better; whilst out with all the family on a pleasant walk along the riverbank, he came across a slide which was intended for a dramatic entrance to the water. Ignoring the fact that he could not swim he of course decided that this would be good fun and duly climbed up, slid down and proceeded to cause absolute chaos as my father and others jumped in to rescue him. I have been told that my dad, as was usually the case, was apoplectic with rage at Neil destroying a relaxing Sunday afternoon stroll, but that was my brother all over.

Strangely, we never argued, never fell out, though I am sure I tested his patience to the full, but my brother never judged me, that is why I always had the utmost respect for him and that is also why I miss him so much now that he is no longer around. Did I place him on a pedestal, I am not sure, but I certainly was very proud of everything he did. Being six years older than me we were never going to have the same problems siblings who are closer in age have. Neil would always include me in things he would do, even when he was in the Sixth Form and I was a First Former as they were called then, I well remember listening to the Moody Blues and playing the Waddington board game 'Formula One' with a few of his friends.

As Neil grew older dad bought him a Motor Scooter and he was very rarely around, I think he fancied himself as a bit of a 'Mod' and he wore a Parka, but he didn't take the Mods vs Rockers scene very seriously. I do remember however that he used to fall off his machine quite regularly, mainly because there were no drink drive laws in those days and it was not unknown for him to ride home intoxicated. Mum would often find him asleep in the porch with his Scooter on the lawn and when he learned to drive he wasn't much better, instead of the Scooter on the lawn it would be his car! They were different times, difficult to understand now in times of the many rules and regulations we have to keep us safe on the road.

Neil went off to Nottingham University when he was 18 and life at home changed for the better really as he and dad had quite a strained relationship which pretty much continued until dad passed away, though there is no doubt that he was very proud of what Neil achieved in his life. dad treated me very differently to Neil, being such a wanted child after losing three babies I was loved unconditionally whatever I got up to and whatever I did in life. I am not sure how Neil felt about this, but he never seemed to resent the attention I got and I was never a rebel, being so like mum I was very easy-going and gave my parents very little trouble.

After his degree he got a job with Unilever, and then moved to St Ivel before joining Schwartz McCormick. He eventually took the post of Director of Sales for a joint venture between his company and Kutas in Turkey which meant a move abroad. Our father had passed away some time ago, but Neil often wished that he was around to see how well he had done, there was always that drive and a need to impress dad, despite the fact he had died seven years ago.

This was a fantastic opportunity for him, but came at a time of great change in our personal lives as our wonderful mother who had continued to live in the family home in Wales was diagnosed with cancer. With Neil in Turkey it fell to me to organise the various details of a care home, visits, and eventually a funeral. There was her house to sort out and sell and together Neil and I spent 3 days together clearing it out. This turned out to be a very emotional but truly bonding experience as we went through the many items mum and dad had acquired over the years. Staying close by in a hotel we went through their belongings during the day either throwing things into a skip or packing to take with us. In the evenings we had a meal and chatted about our lives together and with mum and dad, we had a great time, with lots of laughs and a few tears, but it was a special time and I will always remember it.

Never in each other's pockets, we nevertheless kept in contact whenever we could and with Neil working for an American Company it meant he was abroad a lot so I was used to the mobile phone calls from whichever country he happened to be in at the time. One such call though I remember with absolute clarity coming, as it did, on a sunny evening way back in the summer of 2010, whilst playing cricket for the staff team. Having batted first, I found myself fielding, as usual, way out on the boundary and contemplating life in general.

As I glanced over towards the boundary edge I noticed my wife's car coming along the driveway much faster than she normally would. She parked up and waved towards me, so I jogged over to meet her feeling more and more worried.

"You need to ring your brother now" she said, and by the look on her face I knew it was serious. "What's up" I asked, but Annie was adamant I needed to speak to him. I grabbed my phone and rang, listening intently to the dial tone as it connected to my brother in Turkey. Selfishly I considered the cost of an international call from my mobile, but dismissed that immediately, Neil was my only brother and he needed to speak to me.

"Hi John" my brother spoke in rather tremulous tones, "I have a tumour in my spine" he went on and suddenly I felt the urge to sit down.

I struggled to take in this news, my brother couldn't have a tumour, that sort of thing happened to other people?

"They are going to operate as soon as possible and take a sample to determine if it is cancerous or not, but it is most likely to be benign, so don't worry"

I remember the conversation, or rather the phone call, as everything else was a blur. We exchanged pleasantries and some banter as only brothers can, but really we avoided the obvious, that this was serious. We gave our goodbyes and I wished him well with the operation with a promise to fly over and see him if possible. Turning to Annie, who already knew, I didn't know what to say. Tears welled up in my eyes and we hugged and then I trotted off to finish the game, trying to concentrate as well as I could, but my mind was elsewhere.

Hi John,
Yesterday was the best I felt, although I had a swollen foot and am on anti-inflammatory drugs. But I am stronger walking and think I will try a gentle swim in the pool today for the first time, its 3 weeks since the operation. I have lost some weight, 92 kg now, but appetite slowly returning. Going to see a specialist Oncologist on Thursday to ask more about next steps.

The first operation appeared to have been a success and Neil was soon discharged and back at his house in Turkey recovering. I planned to fly out to Turkey to see him as soon as I finished work for the summer holidays and managed to get a flight out to Izmir with Thompson. Not the best of flights, but it was reasonably cheap and it was good to see Neil at the airport walking, albeit rather stiffly.

I spent five days with Neil and his wife Linda and although it was obvious the operation had taken quite a toll on him, he was as positive as always. There was no talk of any cancer at this stage, not for one minute did we ever think that this tumour would eventually kill him and the time was spent planning ahead. Neil was due to retire at some stage, but he had put it off a few times as he really loved his job, plus living in Turkey was proving to be quite an experience.

We finished the week with a boat trip out to some of the smaller islands with Neil enjoying a bit of fishing as well as a swim in the bay. It was noticeable how difficult he found getting back onboard the boat, which did concern me.

2 CANCER

It would be fair to say that life changed dramatically for my brother that day, dreams of retirement and travel were put on hold as he began the fight of his life, one that he would ultimately lose, but one that he fought bravely and, incredibly, with humour but that was Neil. There followed a series of operations and numerous stays in hospital in a desperate attempt to halt the spread and prolong his life, but this was a very aggressive form of cancer and after radiology was unsuccessful he was told the outcome was terminal within a year. He lost the use of his legs in November, eventually becoming paraplegic from the waist down and confined to a wheelchair.

Neil loved his cars, he was a real petrol head, something we had in common, although he could afford far superior cars to me. He had a number of high performance cars during his lifetime, though always understated, I had the sports cars which were less so! After the diagnosis in June he bought himself a very fast, very flash Audi in Fire Engine Red with the intention of enjoying the freedom of the road whilst he could. Unfortunately that proved to be a very short time and pretty soon he was unable to drive which was one of the hardest things he had to come to terms with. I remember watching the Audi salesman come and drive the car away as Neil sat in his wheelchair with tears rolling down his cheek, a very poignant moment.

As the cancer took hold Neil endured many indignities, the loss of his independence was one thing, but becoming doubly incontinent was very hard for him, but again he treated it with a sense of humour that was inspirational to those around him. Both of us were big fans of Monty Python, though Neil knew many of the sketches better than I did, being particularly proficient at a fake French accent in reciting parts of the quest for the Holy Grail. He would wear a badge with the words "I'm not dead yet" from that infamous film and again could quote verbatim all the words. One of his favourites was the discussion between King Arthur and a peasant:

"Listen, strange women lyin' in ponds distributing swords is no basis for a system of government. Supreme executive power derives from a mandate from the masses, not from some farcical aquatic ceremony".

It would never fail to make us laugh and we would quote words from that particular scene to each other, though I'm not sure our families really understood why we found it so funny? There was always humour with anything Neil did, that was where we shared a common bond, the absurdities of life always made us chuckle and one which we also shared with our father, who despite appearances to the contrary also had a wicked sense of humour.

I don't think Neil ever thought he was going to die, not for one second, and his final months were still one of hope, yet we never ever discussed that issue, I'm not sure why? How do you talk about the end of your life, it is not an easy subject. Our father dropped down dead suddenly of an Aneurysm, there was no time to talk with him and I do regret, like most sons, that I never made the time to talk to him about his early life, it was a missed opportunity and one I will never have again.

In our mother's case, she spent six months in a care home before she's passed away and there were numerous visits, but she was suffering from dementia unfortunately and so the opportunity never arose. In her more lucid moments however she spoke of having had a good life and she was prepared for death, Neil was not ready, he was only 61 when he died, far too young.

I visited my brother a week before he died and it was a very emotional time, he was not really aware of much that was going on although there were some funny moments as I talked to him about our lives together and Neil responded with a memory. It was hard to understand him as his speech was very slurred, the tumour had travelled to his head at this stage and made talking and eating difficult. I hugged him for the last time, knowing then that I would never see him again, I tried not to cry as I held him, but emotions were running high, I was saying farewell to my brother.

There were tears in the car on the way home and the next few days I was expecting a phone call at any time. Remarkably and this is indicative of his incredible spirit, he rallied for a few days, but his body could take no more and on Sunday, a week after I last saw him, he passed away. It was a very cold day when we buried Neil, but the church was absolutely packed as people came from all over to pay their last respects. I found it comforting that a lot of our cousins were there and we shared a lot of memories from the days when we were growing up and would spend a lot of time together. They were fun times and there was a lot of laughter, just what Neil would have expected.

During his illness Neil had determined to do as much as he could in the time that he had and with the help of friends and family, set about raising funds for Cancer Research UK. It was this determination that inspired me to somehow raise money for the same organisation and as I had been, and still was, reasonably athletic in my youth I thought that running the London Marathon would be a challenge that I could undertake. I applied for a place through Cancer Research UK and then waited to hear if I had been successful, not really knowing what I had let myself in for.

Dear John,

Here is an update on my situation since the Operation a month ago. I had another MRI scan today, saw the 2 neurosurgeons that did the Operation and a top Tumour specialist to talk about the findings and the Pathology report I received 3 weeks ago. The scan showed there could be some residual or recurring material there; they are not 100 % sure. But with the Pathology result indicating a recurring (not spreading) malignant tumour it's likely to grow again. Not life threatening but quality of life threatening .The only cure is more surgery, radiation may be possible but it reduces the chances of successful surgery.

I arrived back in the UK feeling a little uneasy about my brother's condition, his body was not responding as well as he would have wished and quite clearly all was not well, but neither of us spoke about the problems he was having. We assumed that recovery was going to be a slow process.

After receiving the latest email from Neil it was clear that the tumour was unfortunately malignant, but not perceived as life threatening, just life changing. Neil was remaining positive however although decisions on retirement and staying in Turkey were obviously now on hold. Again, it never crossed our minds at this stage that this was the beginning of the end.

3 CONFIRMATION OF MY PLACE.

At the beginning of October I received the news that I had got a Golden Bond place with Cancer Research UK which was fantastic news, but pretty much brought it home to me that this was real and my journey had begun. Even though I was a quite sporty when I was younger, running was not really my thing, but I had run a few 5K and 10K races and even the Portsmouth half marathon, but running distances did not come easily to me and so I needed to get some serious training in. 26.2 miles is a long way and I had no idea how my body would react to running such a distance let alone cope with the training.

There was a lot of information available to first time marathon runners like myself and one piece of advice was to join a web site called Real Buzz which was an online community of like-minded people who would be able to help with advice and tips. I signed up at the end of October not really expecting too much, but looking forward to some answers to the many questions I had. Little did I know that signing up that day would have such a profound effect on my life and I would become part of the most incredible support team of the most inspirational people it has ever been my pleasure to know?

My intention initially was to blog about my training purely as a record of my experience of running the London marathon which I thought might be interesting to read afterwards and in years to come. I blogged about every training session sometimes about the run, sometimes about how I was feeling and as the months went by I began to also read what other people were blogging about which was fascinating and useful in equal measure. Pretty soon people would comment and give advice or congratulate and I would comment on their pages. I noticed people began to follow me and I did the same and as the months went by there was a growing bond between us. Even though we had never met we all felt like good friends united in our efforts.

Although there were many other races, at that time the common goal was the London Marathon in April and pretty soon it began to dominate my life, both in training and in blogging. The following chapters are taken from my blog and chronicle my journey to the Mall which took quite a few unexpected turns to say the least.

From: Neil Adam
Sent: Thu, 27th July 2010 18:14
Subject: Neil - Hospital again

Hi John

Arrived back in Oakridge in a bit of a state, pain worse in the back and not passing water properly. Sunday night was a real problem so we called the doctor out and I am now in Frenchay hospital, arrived yesterday. They drained 2.3 litres off from my bladder once they got the tube in and I saw the consultant surgeon after the scan they did when I arrived and they are doing another emergency op tomorrow, the tumour has grown back quickly or they were not able to take it all out first time.

Things took a turn for the worse rather rapidly as my brother endured a very painful trip back from Turkey to his UK home and had to be immediately taken to hospital where they scheduled an emergency op. This unfortunately revealed out worst fears, that the tumour had grown back extremely quickly. As it was wrapped around his spinal cord they were unable to remove all of the tumour initially as it was too dangerous to attempt to do so.

I drove up to the Frenchay hospital in Bristol and Neil was not in good shape, but it was good to see him. He was in surprisingly good spirits, not unusual of course, but this was unknown territory. He had difficulty standing and was quite exhausted, but happy to be in a UK hospital and getting the treatment he needed.

There was no indication at this stage that it was rather more serious than we had hoped although Neil did talk of possibly retiring sooner rather than later. This had been a bit of a wakeup call, though we had no idea just how much of an impact this was going to have.

4 THE EARLY STAGES OF TRAINING

October 25th - A month of running!

Bit late to start this, but felt it would be a good record of my build up to the race. I've been running for just over a month now since I was awarded a place. Started off with running 3 miles three times a week to get used to running on the road. It has been hard, I'm nursing a knee injury, so have to be careful. Racked up 45 miles so far and settled into a sub 10 min a mile pace. I feel that would be a good pace to run at for 26 miles, it feels about right, but some days are easier than others. Ran 6 miles at the weekend in an hour and felt okay, knee was fine, ran 3 miles tonight and felt really good, I suspect my new trainers are run in now as I had no ankle problems, legs didn't feel heavy and breathing was fine.

I was worried that I had taken on too much, but after tonight I feel more positive about the race. Long way to go yet, but feeling much healthier and I have lost over a stone in weight too!

October 27th - It's cold!

The weather has taken a turn for the worst, it was fine jogging in my light weather gear in balmy October sunshine (I did once venture out in the rain) but this is different. What to wear? Don't want to freeze as soon as I get outside, neither do I want to overheat later on in the run. I think a woolly hat may help, I can always take it off to let the heat escape!

Could be a whole new ball game in terms of motivation now it is wetter, colder, darker and probably windy to boot. I have also read, with some trepidation I might add, the different types of training plans people are using. Due to a rather troublesome knee I am subscribing to short runs of 3 to 6 miles up until Christmas to build up stamina. I won't attempt any really long runs until after Christmas and then I probably will only try a 20 mile run once before VLM. From what I have read, this is possible, it's just not the way most people do it, but I want to get to the start line in good health and I am not worried about the time, I just want to finish. So, kit on, cold or no cold, off we go........

October 29th Needed to run, did not want to run......

I really did not want to run today as my ankles were clicking a bit and I had a bad run on Saturday. This was mainly due to RunKeeper going mad and telling me I was running at world record pace for each mile which confused me no end and put me off. I had no idea how far I had run or what pace I was running at. I felt okay, just a bit disorientated, but turns out I ran nearly 5 miles quite comfortably, just not sure of the time.

Anyway, my wife ran the Great South run yesterday, so inspired I thought I would try for a longer run this week. I just didn't feel right, but it turns out I was in good form and felt great for the first few miles, really stretching out and running well under my usual pace until.......... in the dark a kerbstone caught me unawares and I went my length! Apart from my dignity, no damage was done and I continued on my way, but the rhythm was lost. I was gutted as I felt I would try for 10 miles. I ran for just over an hour for a distance of 7 miles, which was pleasing enough and I don't hurt anywhere, ankles are fine, knee is good, just some grazes on my hand.

Such a shame as I was on course for a sub 1:30 10 miles which I would have been pleased with at this stage of my training. Still, can't complain, feel much better than I did back in September when I first started training and reading other people's blogs has really helped

From: Neil
Sent: Wed, 29 July 2010
Subject: Latest news

ʃ

Hi John,

Should be out by Weds and then Radiotherapy can be as an outpatient locally, probably in Glos. They think there might be some damage to my bladder but hope it will recover. They also hope the radiotherapy will hold it back but radical surgery means cutting more out and doing more damage, which can then recover over a period of time, a bit scary! But for now the lower back pain has gone and I can stand up and walk a little.

Neil was still in hospital, but obviously feeling rather better and of course he had access to email through his Blackberry which kept him entertained. Things were looking positive and at this stage we began to believe that things would be okay, the tumour would respond to radiation and all would be well. As the back pain had gone and he was able to walk Neil was much more positive about the long term prognosis although he clearly realised the seriousness of the matter.

It was clear that he continued to plan ahead as he talked about the house project he had on the go and the holidays he and Linda had organised. This was the old Neil, always making plans and organising his life in advance, he loved to have a project on the go, sometimes more than one and would often talk me through an idea with the help of drawings, sketches and magazines.

5 RUNNING IN THE COLD

November 1st - Lovely weather for training!

Despite the tremendous downpour last night the sun is now out so I'm looking forward to a short run later on. After Mondays tumble I'm only running 3 miles, but at a good pace, although I have eaten more this last few days and wonder how this might affect me. I've been eating healthily and with the running and cycling have dropped over a stone, but I don't want to lose much more. Having said that, my knee is not so troublesome now that I am lighter and my running is style is not so laboured. This, combined with the many positive stories on here has really served to increase my confidence in being able to finish the VLM and finish in a good time.

I'm going to continue to cycle every day to work and back and run a couple of times a week as well, this seems to be working for me, but I do like to get out and run, despite the weather. Booked a hotel near the start of the VLM yesterday, thought it best to be rested before the run and not have to drive up or get the train. So I have booked into a hotel less than mile from Greenwich Park, but was horrified at how the prices have been inflated! Most hotels are now full, so I'm glad to have got a room. From what I have read, this seems to be a good idea, hope so!

November 3rd - Pace setting?

Went for a run the other day with my wife and as she is a slower than me the first mile was very comfortable. She did a short run just to get her legs working after the Great South Run she did at the weekend, so I carried on. Realising I was running well below my usual pace I started to wind it up a bit and finished 3 miles in my usual time feeling really good. Today I did the same run on my own, but started at a much quicker pace and felt bad after just a mile and a half. Kept it going, but felt so much different at the end of three miles than previously, yet the times were identical?

Obviously I need to learn to start slowly and build up steadily until I reach a comfortable pace; otherwise I will never make the finish line! Still, back on the bike next week, cycling to work and back each day and a few runs in between. I aim to complete a 10 mile run before the end of the month and feel that is easily within my reach, but I must start slowly.......

November 8th - Bit of a setback.

So Saturday night and Sunday morning were spent experiencing the best that Norovirus has to offer. Managed to lose a whole six pounds in 48 hrs. despite a desperate attempt to stay hydrated. Felt like eating something on Tuesday and finally felt reasonable today. So, back in the saddle, set off for an easy 5k wondering how it would be?

Didn't need to worry, set off steadily and slowly increased my pace, settling into a 9:20 per mile pace. Knee was fine, lungs okay, never laboured and legs didn't feel heavy. Very pleased with that as I was worried I maybe too weak of have a reaction after being so ill. Cycling every day and running as and when I can, I feel I'm on track for the VLM in April. Aiming for a ten mile run before the end of the month, hopefully in around 90 minutes.

November 11th - Winter Running

Now is the time to get in some mileage I suppose, though I am still going for shorter runs at the moment. I am trying to get my body used to a particular pace and it seems to be working as I instinctively know if I am too slow or too fast for what I have worked out to be a reasonable marathon pace.

I seem to settle into a 9:20 sec per mile pace every time I go out and this is a comfortable pace that I can keep up for ten miles easily, just not sure about the other 16, but I am not going to do any long runs until after Christmas and then only one. I figure I have enough miles of training to make it to the end, but time will tell.

My lungs and heart seem to cope well now, my legs are no longer heavy during the run and I feel okay just plodding along to my music and ticking the miles off. I realise I need to take on fluids as I run further, so will take a bottle with me soon, plus some jelly babies!!

All in all, as well as the cycling, I am enjoying the training, but need to stay clear of anything that may cause an injury, so I am not pushing myself too much at this stage. Being able to run continuously for 90 minutes though is a good start!

November 13th - Wow, hit the wall!!!

Felt quite good tonight and I had set myself the target of a 10 mile run before the month was out, so I set off reasonably slowly and built up to a comfortable 9;20 per mile pace. As the miles ticked by I began to think about running 10 miles, but thought I would see how I felt around 6 and 7 miles. It was all going quite well, but I had only set off with the intention of running 3-5 initially, so I didn't take any water with me.

Big mistake, having felt quite fresh after 6 miles, I pushed on but around 8.5 miles I suddenly started to feel bad and my legs felt like lead. I pushed on to 9.5 miles and then had to stop for a stretch out before my legs seized up. After 30 seconds of stretching I carried on to finish the 10 miles in 1 hour 40 minutes.

Not bad, but it was a wakeup call on many levels. I must hydrate during my runs and after some rest days and some shorter runs I will need to push up the mileage to see how my body copes. That was the furthest I have run in twenty years however so I am reasonably pleased, but my body's reaction was not what I expected having been so comfortable over 7 miles previously. Still, that is what the training is for!

November 17th - Back in the saddle

So after my last run went so horribly wrong I allowed myself some rest before venturing out again. I felt quite bad for a couple of days afterwards, not surprisingly as I lost nearly 3 pounds in fluid and obviously needed to rehydrate straight after the run, which I didn't really do.

Anyway, I set off slowly today for a gentle 3 mile run to get the legs going again and settled into a 9:30 pace quite easily. After two miles I was feeling much better and running a little too quickly, so eased back to finish in just under 30 minutes with no ill effects.

Started stretching before AND after now to ease any muscle pains and this seems to be working well. I am making sure I am eating the right foods too and although I don't really start my marathon training until January, I feel I am in a good place now to start building up the mileage.

My "pack" from Cancer Research UK arrived this week too, shirt is rather large so they are sending me another one, and I got my sponsor form out to colleagues at work. I also sent round a link to my just giving page and within a couple of hours my total was up to nearly £400.00, but I have to raise £2000.00, so a long way to go yet! Still, it seems much more real now.

November 25th - Put my back out!

I've not been able to run this week as my back went after my last run on Tuesday somehow. I had to get past somebody walking on the pavement in front of me and stepped off into the road and jarred my back tripping over something. My fault really, I do suffer from a bad back, but running usually keeps problems at bay. I hate to stop when running and although people usually give you room to run past, this person didn't and forced me into the road. It was dark and I didn't see whatever it was I stumbled over.

It was sore when I got back, but the next morning had stiffened up and I couldn't even get my socks on! It has eased and I fancy a run today whilst it is sunny and not chucking it down with rain. We shall see if it is good enough to withstand the pounding of the pavements, but if not I will walk.

I must stretch beforehand however and afterwards AND take water with me. Funny how it becomes quite frustrating when you can't run, it has become like a drug now and I get quite down when I am not able to run. It's all a learning curve before the real training starts in January, I need to listen to my body as I must arrive at the start line in good health and these problems are something I need to learn how to avoid in the run up to the VLM in April.

November 25th - My back was fine!

Ran three miles fairly easily, no problem with the back, though good knee was starting to hurt a bit so I eased up. Still managed a consistent 9:30 a mile pace though, so quite pleased.

November 27th - Nothing hurt?

So I wondered about going out today after some niggling aches and pains on Sunday? Cycled to work and back into tremendous winds and felt like I had done quite a workout when I got back. Decided to go for a three mile run, usual route and see how things felt. Got round remarkably easily, no aches from either knee, ankles okay, breathing fine and settled into a 9:30 pace, which seems okay at the moment.

Saw a consultant on Monday about my knee and he has referred me for a scan at last. It has been troubling me for around four years now and I have had physiotherapy, an x-ray and now hopefully the scan will reveal what I think is just wear and tear. If I need an operation to clean out the knee, then I will take that option as long as it is not too close to the VLM. I can run okay, it is just sore during and after, although less so since I have lost weight? If anybody has had an arthroscopy then I'd be grateful for some information as to how it went and recovery period?

November 30th - It is seriously cold for running!

Well it is for a soft southerner! Went out tonight and it was mightily cold, -2 apparently and it felt very different. Breathing was difficult so I decided to take it easy to begin with and although I was slower, not by much and I felt good at the end. Just a short three miles to keep the training ticking over until January when I start the 16 week beginners plan!

I cycle for 40 minutes every day except Sunday, but run every two days or so, so I don't feel that I will be unprepared when the mileage starts to go up. It's finding the time that worries me a bit. Running in the morning is not possible, I prefer evening or afternoon runs anyway, but getting back between 6:30 and 7:00 and then doing a 2 hour plus run before stretching, showering and eating should be interesting?

I will do some longer runs at the weekends and keep to short runs during the week I think, got to listen to my body too, a few aches and pains today, but they came and went. Target is still to get to the start line in good health and the finish line between 4 hours and 4 hours 30 minutes. Is it possible, I hope so, but at the end of the day, I'm running for my brother Neil.

Dear John

They did another scan yesterday, and a brain one .There is still quite a bit of tumour there that surgery can't get at. Also there was a small dark patch in another place so they are taking some fluid from my spine on Monday so that they can check if it is in the fluid and design the radiation treatment appropriately .Looks like it may already have spread but they think it's a type that will respond to radiation ok. Pathology report back on Weds to confirm. I'm expecting a long haul now so mentally I'm starting to think about moving back from Turkey to focus on getting this sorted in the UK and not going back to work.

As Neil was back in the UK it seemed that updates on his condition were rather more regular and treatment was more focused on finding out what effects this tumour may have long term and how best to deal with it. As there seemed to be a plethora of tests to endure he had begun to consider his future and the possibility he may have to move back from Turkey and focus on getting his health back.

Still positive and obviously there was still no indication of any long term issues other than having to endure radiotherapy to keep the tumour at bay. Certainly at this stage he, or indeed the rest of the family, had any idea that this was anything more than a problem that was serious, but one that could be dealt with eventually.

6 TRAINING IS GETTING SERIOUS

December 2nd - First 100 miles of training done!

Well that was a nice easy run in the sun, and even though it was cold I seemed to improve my pace running mid-morning. I have also reached the 100 mile mark after a couple of months of training. Not brilliant, but not bad and no injuries as yet. Start the countdown in January with a proper plan to stay healthy, but build up the mileage slowly. Still cycling which is a useful exercise and a welcome break from the runs.

Got my running t-shirt from Cancer Research UK, the one they originally sent me was massive, but this one fits fine. They have let me keep the original so I am using it to train in, reminds me of why I am doing this. I actually don't mind going out in the cold now, just wish I had more time to go for longer runs, but every run helps I guess.

December 4th - Another run in the cold......

Went out tonight with the intention of running 3 miles, but I did over 5 instead and felt good, one of those runs when everything seems to work well. Breathing was good, legs were fine and I kept a comfortable pace going throughout the run, if I can just feel that way on April 21st then I should have no problems. Hopefully the training will give me the confidence to push to the end. Already 5 miles feels like a short run, two months ago 2 miles seemed like a long run, so my perspective has changed at least.

It was cold though and I wrapped up enough to keep the chill out, but not too much so that I got overheated. Have found that after 4 miles I need water, so will start taking a bottle with me, hate running with anything in my hand though, so will have to get used to it. Will also need some sort of food as I get up to 10 miles, not sure what though, seems jelly babies are popular? All in all it was a good run and I feel positive, but there seems to be lots more to think about as the mileage increases!

December 8th - Running with a cold, in the cold!

Some runs are harder than others, I have a cold, sore throat, cough and feel tired, but after cycling home after work I managed to get out for a 3 mile run. It wasn't easy as my breathing was difficult, but my pace was good. I wonder if I should have gone out, but I feel guilty if I don't. After a long hot shower I promptly fell asleep for a couple of hours and this was mid-afternoon! Feel much better now, must listen to my body, but still managed the run okay. I'm averaging around 12 miles a week running and 25 miles a week cycling and I'm not losing weight anymore. My diet hasn't changed, although I have had a few mince pies :-)

I'm pleased with the training so far and in January I hope to get some longer runs in. Hopefully I have given myself a good base which will carry me through to April and the VLM.

December 12th - Sub-zero temperatures!!

Went for a run today and it was incredibly cold! I tried to go as early in the evening as possible to avoid the ice, but at 5:00pm the paths were well and truly iced over. Breathing was again difficult, but I was well wrapped up and in no danger of overheating! Steady 3 miles at a good pace, I wanted to get home to the shower as quick as I could. Need to get a long run in this week, 7 to 8 miles or longer if I feel okay, but need to take on water before and after, not too sure about during?

Sponsorship has nearly reached the £500 mark, so feeling positive as well, but still £1500 to go, need a big push after the Christmas break and in the month leading up to the run. Serious training starts on the 1st January, but I feel as if I am in good shape, long may that last!

December 13th - Runkeeper going crazy?

Did a 4 mile run in a positively balmy 2 degrees! Well I thought I did, but it told me I was running a 6 min mile pace and had done half a mile before I had even got going! It is a right pain not knowing what pace I am doing as I rely on it for checking my times and distances. It has been fairly consistent showing anything from 9:20 to 9:40 mile pace, but seems to have jumped to around 9:00 a mile now. Now either I am much fitter and running quicker or it is lying! I know that my music is 30 minutes long and I know the markers for each mile on my route, but it is confusing me no end. I will give it one more go and if it doesn't work I will look for an alternative method of checking my pace, distance and time.

The run was okay, steady pace throughout, bit of stomach cramps and some twinges in my hips, but nothing too bad. Looking forward to the weather warming up, it has been really hard to get out and run in the cold.

December 16th - Set off to do 10 miles.......

Some runs are just bad for whatever reason? I set off in good spirits to run 10 miles and maybe push on for longer, but it became obvious after 3 that it was going to be a struggle to do half that. My knees are playing up a bit, but although my breathing was fine, my legs felt very heavy, which I can only put down to a day of indulgence the day before. It was a corporate Christmas lunch and I ate quite a large meal, but drunk sensibly. Even so, I thought it might affect my run today and it seemed to, though I am concerned about my knees. I was managing the left knee quite well, but now the right knee has started to hurt a bit and both remain sore long after the run.

I hope this is not going to be a problem? I will do some shorter runs during the week and see how they feel, but I really want to get one more long run in before the marathon training starts in January. However, if my knees are going to be a problem I may have to restrict myself to short runs and bike rides to maintain my core fitness and then hope for the best on the day!

I have a scan on my left knee at the end of the month and hopefully I will finally find out what the problem is. If I do need some sort of op, I will probably defer to after the VLM, but I can't see that being a problem as no doubt I will be on a waiting list for 6 months or more! Here's hoping it is just wear and tear and some rest and a couple of light runs will improve the situation.

December 18th - Typical!

After Sunday I was a bit worried about running this week, but felt I needed to try the knees out and see how it went. It was a lovely day, but I had promised my boys that I would take them to see 'The Hobbit' so I set off with the intention of running 3 miles only. Typical that the knees were fine and I felt good, so good that would have liked to have carried on, but time was against me so I settled for 4 miles and a better feeling than Sunday!

Would have really liked to have carried on as I wanted to run 10 miles on Sunday. Never mind, my knees aren't sore, the pace was good and I felt fine. Odd how some runs are better than others, but I am getting better at listening to my body and easing back the pace when I need to. Today was a good day; I really hope April 21st is also a good day!

December 20th - One day I will experience a perfect run..........

Gentle run today and I was able to experiment with my running style a bit. Even so, I don't think I have managed any run without something being wrong. Initially it was a lack of fitness and heavy legs, then lungs on fire, heart beating fast, ankles hurting, knee hurting, hips aching, nose running, or all of them at the same time! Just once I would like to experience a run when everything is working properly and I feel good to run Forrest Gump like into the distance.

Anyway, maybe with more training that day will come, but until then I am fit enough now to experiment with my style, tempo etc. tried bounding a bit more today and it felt okay, pace was good and I am slowly formulating a VLM plan to get me through the run. I realise that the start will be slow due to sheer numbers and so have started much slower than my ordinary pace. I've noticed that after 30 minutes of running I settle into a comfortable 9:30 per mile pace and feel reasonably good. Hopefully that will continue for quite a few miles, but I do need to get in another long run before the real training starts in January, though I must remember to hydrate.

December 22nd - Running in the rain!

I wasn't looking forward to running in the rain today and it was lashing it down for hours, but finally it eased enough for me to head off out. I set off with the intention of running 5 miles, but settled into a good rhythm around 20 minutes into the run so decided to run 6 miles or maybe more? Seems whatever I do, 9:30 per mile is 'my pace' and nothing I do to slow down or speed up makes any difference! After around 5 miles I started to think about doing 10, but around 6 my right knee started to hurt a bit. I carried on hoping it would ease, but the heavens opened and it really began to rain. Being not far from home at this stage I decided to run for just an hour and made my way back for a hot shower.

I am a little worried by my knees, the left one has been a problem for a while now, but the right is now displaying similar issues although it never stops me running, they are just sore for a while during and after the run. I've heard of runners' knee, but I'm not sure that's what I am experiencing? Will go for a shorter run on Christmas Eve and then rest up for a couple of days and see how the knees are. Hopefully it is just something I can work through without too much trouble?

December 24th - Last run before the festivities begin!

After a couple of late nights and rather too much food and drink I set off this morning for an easy 5k with some trepidation! I had strapped both knees this time and it seemed to do the trick as they were fine. I settled into my usual 9:30 pace and completed the 5k in under 30 minutes with no real problems, but I was conscious that my diet over the last few days had rather a detrimental effect on my running as I did feel quite sluggish.

I have learnt so much about how my body reacts to running this last few months and I am now trying to work out how best to fuel for the longer runs. I have also been stretching more, especially my ankles which are a problem in the first 5-10 minutes of a run. It has been quite a steep learning curve, but I feel much more positive about completing the VLM in a reasonable time, particularly after reading the various blogs on here which have been very helpful.

Merry Christmas everybody and here's hoping for an injury free New Year!

December 26th - Boxing Day run, 10 miles and no wall this time :-)

At last, a decent run and felt fine throughout, we'll almost as I had to pop back home for the loo! I had some new running gear, gloves, beanie, socks plus some hydration packs. Set off to run 5k at first, but felt good so changed my route to 10k. I was trying to run at a slower pace and that seemed to work? Anyway, as I got closer to 10k I felt I could manage 10 miles, but I was desperate for the loo at this stage. As I was close to home after 7 miles I popped in and went straight back out to complete 10.25 miles in 1 hour 40 minutes.

I am quite pleased with that as the last time I hit the wall at 9.5 miles, badly! The socks were a big help as we're the hydration packs, so I feel good about moving up to half marathon distance. My knees seem okay, I wasn't struggling to breathe and my legs did not feel heavy, although they ache now!

Advice on here has been invaluable; somebody mentioned running two loops and popping in for a drink at the halfway stage as they hate carrying anything. Me too, can't stand to run with anything in my hand, so this morning's run was perfect in that respect. Just a couple of shorter runs before the New Year begins, and then the proper training starts.

December 28th - Short run, faster pace.

Went for a short run, 5k and easily maintained a faster pace throughout. Clearly my marathon pace is slower at the moment, but maybe it will pick up once I start on my training plan? I'm glad I started running way back in October as it has given me a good base to build on and also my perception of distance has changed, 10k is a short run and 10 miles doesn't seem too far anymore. My next target is to run for 15 miles before the end of January. I am going to try three loops of 5 miles and stop back at my house at the end of each loop for a drink and maybe the loo!

Hopefully that will work without me having to carry any water, although I will take some hydration gel packs with me. Got some Sorbathane insoles today as well, interesting to see how I run with those too, they have come highly recommended, we shall see? Finally, my knee scan is on Monday, maybe I will finally find out if it is a major problem or just wear and tear, but if an operation is needed I will defer until after the VLM as both knees seem to be holding up after over 150 miles of training.

December 30th - Really enjoyed my run today, at last!

Went for a longish run today and really enjoyed it. The sun was out and it was very mild, if a little windy at times. I was trying out my new Sorbathane insoles for my trainers and they seemed to make quite a difference. I tried to keep to my marathon pace of just under 10 minutes per mile, but managed to run 7 miles in just over 66 minutes at a 9:30 pace and felt good. Settled into a good rhythm after 20 minutes and enjoyed the sights around me.

As well as the insoles I had a hydrating drink before the run, new double skin socks and some running gloves, plus a new selection of music to run to! It all seemed to make for a very pleasant run and now that I am happy running for an hour at a reasonable pace I am confident about starting my 16 week training plan on New Year's Day

My aim to run 15 miles by the end of January looks reasonable, but I am going to substitute some runs with bike rides, just to protect my knee. I have to be sensible about the training and not push too hard too soon. Looking forward to the VLM now with much more conviction, I have been reading 'Keep on Running, The Highs and Lows of a Marathon Addict' by Phil Hewitt, which is very entertaining and also very useful. He has run 25 marathons to date, his first being in London and his experiences are a useful reference point for a first timer like me.

He talks about the effect the crowds have and today I realised what a boost that can be. As I started my 7th mile I was hooted by a family I know and waving back I was conscious of how good I felt and how that carried me to the end of the run at a much greater pace, but with less effort it seemed. Whatever the reason though, it made me feel good about what I was doing, just a simple hoot and wave, amazing, and makes me wonder what effect thousands of people cheering you on will have? That's my last run before the New Year, 160 miles covered since I got my place and started training and nearly £600 raised so far.

Happy New Year and Happy Running!

Dear John

I had some bad news again today following my 5 week Radiotherapy treatment and MRI scan a few weeks ago. The tumour is still active and has grown again by approx. 10% since the operation. The effect of this has manifested itself with more numbness in my legs and trunk and in the last few days a return of the back pain .They have put me back on Steroids which should reduce the swelling and pain for now. This tumour is of a type that does not respond to Chemo and is also too embedded in the Spinal cord for more surgery. So there is nothing more now they can do to cure me, only help me be as comfortable as possible. This is an aggressive tumour so it's likely to continue growing and eventually will kill me, timescale unknown but probably much less than a year unless a miracle happens. I am gutted right now.

I think this is quite possibly the most upsetting of all the emails I received from Neil during the course of his illness. He had rung me to let me know the evening before, which was a difficult enough conversation to have, but it was rather bought home to me the next day when written down in black and white. I remember I was thinking of buying a rowing boat to use on the Hamble river near where we live and that maybe when Neil was better we could take a trip out. The news from my brother that night was devastating to say the least and the phone call was a short one. It is difficult to sum up how I felt that night, but impossible to know how Neil must have been feeling.

Those were very dark days indeed and I remember feeling very angry as well as upset. I carried on at work the next day as usual keeping myself busy, but by lunchtime the reality hit me and I went for a walk around the grounds before breaking down in tears. I managed to ring a colleague who organised cover for my next lesson whilst I gathered my thoughts and then returned to teach my last class of the day.

7 INTO THE NEW YEAR

January 1st - First run of the New Year!

Started my 16 week training plan for the VLM today, a nice easy 5k which was welcome, given the late night celebrations. I was accompanied by my eldest son, who will be 16 next month and has decided to get fitter. I ran slowly to ease him in gently, but picked up the pace to around 9:30 a mile as he is quite a bit younger than me! He started to flag around two miles though and headed home after that, leaving me to pick up the pace a bit more and finish strongly at around 9:00 a mile pace. I am going to attempt the really short runs at a faster pace now and really push towards working harder. The longer runs I will settle into my marathon pace, but I need to try some interval training as well.

Feeling very positive as well, I have never felt this good on January 1st, which is no doubt due to the training I have done since I got my place. I have also eaten well and drunk less! Everything is focussed towards April 21st now and getting there in good shape, it all seems much more real somehow?

January 3rd - It had to happen!

Well I should have been doing my second run today of 6 miles, but for the first time an injury has prevented me from running. I jarred my back avoiding a car on my last run, running rage, and it seized up last night which meant I was very stiff and sore this morning. I'm gutted as things were going well. On the plus side, a day laid up with painkillers and hot packs on the affected area have worked wonders (note to self, the next time my back goes, do not struggle into work, rest) and I think I will be okay to run tomorrow.

I also rewarded myself with a Garmin 110 which should arrive tomorrow, so maybe the rest was meant to be and I can trial it tomorrow, I hope so as I have heard good things about it. Everybody seems to have had a setback or two, so I am in good company, but hopefully I will not get any back problems again before April 21st, going to be very careful!

I am enjoying the training now and so it was hard not to go out today, but I am getting better at listening to my body and rest was definitely needed. The weather is very mild as well, which makes for a pleasant run, so much for the expected cold snap? 107 days to go!

January 4th - Garmin Time!

I was desperate for my back to improve enough to run today, so after a day of stretching and rest I was pleased to wake up with only a slight soreness. Having checked the delivery time I realised my new Garmin was due sometime this morning so decided to stretch and rest and see how I felt.

After it arrived I charged it whilst reading up how to set it all up, which was remarkably easy. I then got changed with the intention of trying it out AND seeing how my back was. I hit a slight snag however as fully kitted out in my running gear and the Garmin on my wrist I realised I couldn't actually read it without my glasses! I never run with my glasses on, but it never occurred to me that I would need them for looking at a watch, how stupid of me!

Thinking I might have to send it back, it occurred to me that I had set everything up whilst wearing my glasses and so taking them off to run meant I was suddenly looking at the Garmin in a dark porch and my eyes were not adjusting to the change. Therefore, once I was out in full daylight I had no trouble in pressing the right buttons and seeing what my pace, time and distance were throughout what turned out to be a 5 mile run.

My back was fine and running helps anyway, but I felt no twinges at all so settled into trying out my 5 mile loop which I intend to do three times with drink stops before January is over. I felt okay, but worryingly my pace was a lot quicker than Runkeeper had been telling me? I presume that the Garmin is far more accurate which means I have been running at a much quicker pace than I previously thought.

Time will tell, but the run was good, just over 44 minutes for 5 miles and no problems at all, plus the data uploaded to Runkeeper very easily and that is shared to my Facebook for my friends and family to see how my training is going. So, I am pleased with my back issues, pleased with my run and very pleased with my Garmin which has proven to be everything I wanted and more. Back on track, long run on Sunday and then back to work on Monday, happy running everybody.

January 6th - Longer run and time to think!

Third run of my marathon training plan and I wanted to go for 8 miles this time. Sundays will be my long runs, building up to 15 miles by the end of the month. Week days I will cycle every day to work and back and run some shorter runs every other day. Shorter being 3-5 miles and longer being 8 miles upwards; getting serious now!

I had in mind my 5 mile loop, passing my house for a drink and then a further 3 miles to finish. In a couple of weeks' time I want to be able to run 2 of the 5 mile loops with a drink in between, hopefully anyway. I set off at a slightly slower pace and settled in nicely to a 9:10 pace which was kept up for the first 4 miles and then I headed back to my house for a much needed drink. I haven't worked out how to pause my Garmin if indeed it does, so opening my porch to retrieve and consume a gel pouch reduced my pace somewhat.

Anyway, I set off on the last stretch with no problems and enjoyed the sights and sounds of people going about their business on a Sunday morning. It was nice to be able to run without too much discomfort and think about things that I wanted to do.

I started to tire around 7 miles however, due I think to hydration, I must drink more, but I pushed onto 8 miles and home. It took me around 76 minutes in total for an average pace of 9:27, slower than my last run, but I did stop for a drink although I'm not sure if that would make much difference to be honest and I'm happy with my run.

Whilst I was running I started to think about a format for the book I am hoping to write. It has been quite a journey since we first received the news of my brother's illness and I would quite like to write about what has lead me to train and run the London Marathon. With many hours of training ahead of me I have plenty of time to think and plan, but essentially it will be a tribute to my brother Neil whose life was so cruelly cut short. He is my inspiration when the going gets hard as I know that however much I am suffering it is nothing to what he had to endure.

January 9th - Furthest and fastest 30 min run.

Missed my run yesterday nursing a sore back, but it doesn't seem to hinder me running so ventured out today. My weekday runs are shorter, but faster, so I upped the pace a bit. Surprised myself by running nearly 3.5 miles in 30 minutes and at the end my pace was just a tad over 8 minutes per mile which I was really pleased with. My knee and back were fine, although the back is a bit sore at the moment, but I was never struggling. This should, apparently make the longer runs easier as I will be running at a slower pace for longer, we shall see?

I am a bit concerned about my back, I am mobile again and not feeling as if it could go again at any minute, but it is very sore to the right of my lower lumbar region? I am not sure whether to see a physiotherapist, chiropractor or osteopath or if it will ease eventually? It doesn't stop me running, in fact running has always improved my bad back, but this feels different.

Whatever it is I do need to get it looked at if it doesn't improve in the next week. Pleased with everything apart from that and looking forward to my long run on Sunday when I hope to step up to 10 miles for the third time and maybe longer if I feel okay.

January 13th – Cramp

Today was a first in more ways than one! Set off to do 10 miles or more, but taking it steady to see if I could maintain a more relaxed pace. It was all going well until about 5 miles when I suddenly got some pain in my right calf which was bearable but annoying as things were going well. I then started to feel the same in my left calf and around about 6 miles the pain was quite severe. I had been feeling really good about my pace, breathing etc. and had thought I may be able to loop back home, pick up a drink and then carry on for 12-13 miles in total, certainly a minimum of 10.

At 6.5 miles I had to stop and try and stretch the calves out, but it was too late, so I set off back home to finish with only 8 miles and really sore calf muscles. I drank copious amounts of fluid when I got back and had a long hot bath, but they are still very sore after nearly two hours. It is good to experience this now and make sure it doesn't happen again. I presume it is down to my usual problem of not taking in enough fluid before or during the run, but I have run this far before and not had a problem?

Whatever caused the cramp, I need to make sure I find out what it was as it would be awful if it happened on April 21st. I could just about hobble round, but it is incredibly painful! So, another training problem and one to learn from, but I am so disappointed as I felt really in tune and happy with my pace. Never mind, what doesn't kill us makes us stronger as they say.

January 16th – Setback

Well I've not run since the cramping episode on Sunday, still cycling but my right calf muscle is still a bit sore. Felt reasonable today after some stretching so I ventured out in -2 this evening for 5k. Starting feeling it after less than 5 minutes and eased up a bit but to no avail. Still sore and so worrying about doing more damage I stopped and walked back home feeling quite despondent. Everything feels okay now, but this injury has thrown me a bit as I was just getting into a good training pattern.

I need to rest it I guess, maybe some heat treatment or a massage? I do have some compression socks on the way, hopefully they will make a difference, all the advice I have had says they will. Not much I can do about it, but glad I wasn't far from home and no damage done. I just hope it will clear up quickly as I hate to miss a run, but I'm sure I can make it up next week. Would like to be feeling up to a long run on Sunday, but that may be too soon, we shall see?

January 19th - Back problems again!

I have not run for a week now and really miss getting out, but yesterday, having been sent home early from work due to the snow, I bent down to greet our dog and my back gave out! Managed to get upright in a great deal of pain and spent the rest of the day flat out. So disappointed, but what can I do? Looks like I may be off running for some time now until my back settles down. Work on Monday looks unlikely as I can't even stand up without some real difficulty.

May have to get the doctor out if I can't move easily, but definitely need to see a physiotherapist as this is the second time this has happened in a month. Obviously running is placing some sort of strain on my back and I need sorting out and quickly too! It might be my trainers or the way I run, but it needs sorting out with just three months to go.

So here I am, laid up in bed with a heat pad on my back and unable to move without a lot of pain. Just standing up feels like someone thrusting a knife into my lower back and getting dressed takes a long time, so frustrating. To add insult to injury, my compression socks arrived as well, but at least my calf is being rested, the only positive I can see at the moment. To be honest there is so much snow and ice around at the moment that I doubt I could have got out for a run anyway this weekend, but it is disappointing, especially as training was going well and I was moving into double figures for mileage quite easily.

Hopefully this will not be a major setback and I can get back onto my training plan very soon, just doesn't feel that way at the moment.

January 21st - Physiotherapy today

My mobility has improved since I started using ice packs and Biofreeze, but my back was still very sore. So I was looking forward to my trip to the physiotherapist today, although having suffered at the hands of a chiropractor, or was it an osteopath, I was a little unsure. However I was pleasantly surprised and after experiencing some pretty impressive manipulation I feel pretty good. I have never heard or experienced so much clicking of joints, obviously my muscles were in knots!

Anyway, I will wait to see if I feel better tomorrow after a night's sleep, but my back feels a lot better at the moment? So, no running yet, but hopefully I will get out for a walk sometime this week and try a gentle jog at the weekend, weather permitting. Suffering with an ear infection at the moment, to add insult to injury! So painful so I probably need to see a doctor tomorrow, really fed up with all these problems and hoping that things will settle down soon. Can't wait to get back running plus I need to sort out some new trainers that will get me round the VLM. Can't do that until I'm running properly again, hopefully next Monday, fingers crossed!

January 24th - Light at the end of the tunnel?

My back is much better now, it would seem that in nursing my left knee I have compensated in my running style which has thrown my back out on the right side. After ice, Ibuprofen and a trip to the physiotherapist it is much better, but not quite sure what to do to prevent it happening again? Obviously I need to get someone to look at how I am running, but I had intended to get down to a highly recommended running outfit who video you and then match you up to the correct footwear. As soon as I am jogging lightly again I will pop down and probably not a moment too soon?

Still have a little bit of earache, but not as bad as it was, although I do seem to be spending quite a lot on medicines and running aids! My compression socks have arrived, though I have had no chance to wear them as yet. Hoping to get out at the weekend for a light jog and see how things go and how I feel. Dying to get back to training, although it is very cold at the moment, so not unduly worried. Hopefully I can get back on my bike as well now that the snow and ice have all but gone.

I never considered for one minute that I would have to put up with all these niggles, but I am glad they have come now and not nearer the VLM. Gives me time to sort out the problems and make sure I am doing things right. I must get to the start line as fit and as healthy as I can be.

January 28th - and now Sciatica!

I had 4 hours of feeling pretty good on Sunday and contemplated a light jog to see how things were, then suddenly I started to get a pain to the right of my spine towards my right hip and shooting down my leg. Most uncomfortable and nothing I did would ease the pain. Turns out this is sciatica and is a by-product of my slipped disc a week ago. It is really painful so today was a challenge, but I got through it and am seeing the physiotherapist, again, on Wednesday.

So, from being on track to running 15 miles by the end of this month I have not run for two weeks now and feel a bit despondent. I read on the blogs of people increasing their mileage to the mid-teens and I am worrying that it will be awhile before I am back running again. I have started to comfort eat too and have put on a few pounds which I could well do without.

Hopefully after Wednesday I will be able to think about a run at the weekend, we shall see and I hope that this setback will not prove to be a problem as the days tick by to April 21st. I need to get back out there!!!

January 30th - Good news, bad news!

Bad news first - Well I saw the consultant today about my knee and as expected it is a torn cartilage. I need an operation to repair it, but they won't be able to see me until after the VLM. Running is not a problem, it is just a bit unstable and sore so I'm going to run anyway, but take it nice and steady. I won't be able to do the sort of mileage I wanted to before the marathon or indeed the number of runs as I don't want to do any more damage. However, I have been running with this problem for a long time now, so a few more months will not make much difference and at least I know that I will be seen to afterwards.

The good news is after physiotherapy I feel so much better, the sciatica has eased considerably and I expect to be able to jog lightly at the weekend, but I will go for a couple of long walks beforehand and maybe a cycle. So I'm pleased that I have a diagnosis at last, it has only taken three years from when I first saw a doctor about it. Hopefully the next post will be about a run and not an injury, here's hoping!!

Hi John

Pain is getting worse overnight unfortunately and yesterday walking was difficult, but I did a lot over the weekend Today hope to stay in bed until 11am catching up with lists, mails, calls, telly and Internet! And I have drugs and a support team to get back on track, so it won't stop me pushing the boundaries.

Despite the horrible diagnosis Neil soon revealed just what a determined character he was and there was a positive vibe to his emails and phone calls. Typically he started to plan various activities to keep him busy and as always he expected to go beyond what was expected of him. Very soon there were plans to buy a motorhome and travel through Europe to Turkey as well as numerous outings to places he wanted to visit in the UK.

He was increasing reliant on technology for entertainment and I organised a laptop and wireless printer so that he could surf the Internet and generally keep himself busy. He very much enjoyed the chance to research and purchase items online and of course he was able to keep in contact with his workplace which gave him a purpose still. I guess that was his way of dealing with the knowledge that he had been given a certain amount of time to live and so he filled his days with activities to take his mind of such an awful fact.

8 INJURY PROBLEMS

February 2nd - Cramped again.....

Felt good enough to get back in the saddle and so set off after eating a banana, drinking some water, stretching and massaging the muscles in my bad leg. Felt okay for a mile if a bit out of condition, although my Garmin showed a 9:10 pace which was a bit too fast for a comeback jog. My right leg was feeling odd though, the sciatica has not completely gone, but various exercises have lessened the dull ache I get running from my right hip down my leg.

Then suddenly my right calf cramped up? I stopped straight away this time and gently walked back feeling really hacked off. I don't know if I am ever going to sort this leg out? So iced, hot bath, massage and painkillers taken I'm watching England thrash Scotland and wondering when I will be able to run again.

Going to cycle again to keep my conditioning up and see what can be done, but not feeling very positive at the moment. I'm desperate to get back out there as I should have hit the 15 mile mark by now. Still, I have to take the positive as my back is much improved and I am generally feeling much fitter, yet it is annoying not being able to run when I feel much able to. Time will tell and hopefully this will be a minor setback?

February 6th Still not able to run?

I am getting worried now, it's been four weeks since my last proper run and I am concerned that unless I can get back on the road in the next week or so I will have to defer to next year. This I do not want to do at all, but I have to be realistic. I was ahead in my training and running 10 miles easily, but having lost nearly 4 weeks now I feel as if I will be starting all over again?

The sciatica has eased considerably and I am hoping I can get out this weekend for a light jog without any pain and no cramping. If I can manage that I think that a steady 8 weeks of training will be enough to get me round, but only if I can get running again.

I do hope so as it means so much to me, but then again it has taught me that however bad I have felt, at least I knew I would get better. My brother did not have that luxury as comfortable was the best he could hope for. It's a stark reminder of how fragile we can be and such a simple thing as running has really bought home the delicate balance there is in remaining injury free.

Fingers crossed it all goes well at the weekend, I shall stretch each leg, hydrate and fuel correctly, wear compression socks and take it steady and hopefully by next week I will be getting some miles under my belt again?

February 13th - Decision time?

Saw the doctor on Monday and he gave me some stronger painkillers to try to help with the sciatica. Seemed to help the first day, but I had an uncomfortable night last night, almost like shin splints as the pain made its way from my hip to my shin. It is now a month since my last training run, so today was really decision time.

I stretched carefully, iced, drank and got kitted out for a short trial run. I warmed up first then set off very slowly; the leg was fine, even though it felt tight at the back of the thigh. Then I felt the familiar sensation of tightness in my calf and sure enough, I cramped after half a mile. I walked slowly back wondering if it was something that would release itself, but after trying to jog slowly again it came back at the back of my thigh and the calf.

My running style was back to normal however, I wasn't favouring any leg and I obviously have a core fitness level as I felt fine breathing wise, but I can't run if I am cramping like this every time. I had taken in enough fluid, had compression socks on and had stretched carefully, but because this leg is tight from the sciatica it is obviously affecting my calf too. So, I have to make a decision and soon, should I wait it out, cycle as much as possible and see if the leg improves or should I defer now?

I have no doubt I can run the distance, albeit slower than I would have wanted to, but not unless this leg allows me to run without cramping, therefore I have to ease the sciatica ASAP! Going back to the doctor on Friday if the pills don't appear to ease the situation, but maybe walking, stretching etc. will release whatever is causing me such discomfort.

Here's hoping, I am staying positive, but if I have to defer to next year, then so be it! Happy running everybody, reading your blogs and seeing how well your training is going is inspiring and will also help me make the right decision when the time comes.

February 17th - A cocktail of drugs......

This week, having finally decided that the Naproxen the doctor gave me was not working I went back to the doctor again on Thursday. I never visit the doctor, I can count the number of times over the years on one hand, so three times in less than a week and I'm beginning to feel like a hypochondriac!

Anyway, he examined me in that non-committal way that only doctors can do and concluded that it was indeed sciatica and if the naproxen wasn't helping then he would prescribe me something stronger!

So I have since been taking diazepam and co-codamol as well as the naproxen and spent most of the last few days in a daze! Has it improved my sciatica? Difficult to tell really, I felt no pain the first day and spent most of it in bed spaced out, but since then as my body built more of an intolerance to the pills the pain has gradually returned, albeit slightly less intense. Sleeping has been much better and waking every day I have felt that may be today the pain will have gone, but it still persists.

So I finished off the last of the pills today and after a visit to the physiotherapist yesterday I feel slightly better, I think? I feel fit enough, I can walk okay without shooting pains down my right leg, but can I run? My physiotherapist says I must let my body heal itself, the muscles should have relaxed enough to release whatever is causing the pain, but if so it is taking it's time!

As I write this, I have a dull ache in my right buttock which radiates down through my thigh to my calf, but it does feel different, as if it is releasing itself slowly. The tightness in the back of my thigh seems to have lessened and it is that that causes the cramping in my calf, so hopefully I may be able to try a run tomorrow?

I am going to carry on with the exercises today, stretching and massaging the problem areas and then trying a walk to see how it feels. If all goes well I will try another light jog on Monday afternoon, but if I cramp again I am not sure where that leaves me? I am determined to run the VLM this year, the doctor says the sciatica will go eventually (days, months, years?) and so I will cycle to keep my core fitness up and go for long walks and these activities don't seem to cause cramp at all. Hopefully the sciatica will improve enough for me to start running again and then it will just be a case of a steady jog around 26.2 miles!

Here's hoping I can get this leg sorted and get to the start line on April 21st, the weeks are flying by now and time is running out, but I do feel a little more positive than before, despite the distinct lack of training. It has been great reading other people's blogs however, happy running, good luck to you all; I hope to see you at the start line!

February 20th - Running again.......just!

My sciatica has eased a bit, though it is taking it's time to heal, but I felt okay to try another run and see where I was, both in fitness and conditioning? Stretched as usual, drank and ate a banana before kitting myself out and heading off slowly. Walked and stretched for a bit and then started some light jogging. Hip was a bit sore but that began to ease and I felt quite comfortable for the first mile. I started to feel my calf tighten not long after that so tried to relax and concentrate on my running style. Just after two miles though the calf really started to tighten so I stopped and walked back home slowly.

I can feel the sciatica easing, but that is causing the tightness in the back of my thigh which then transmits down to my calf. I feel fine to run, albeit a bit slower than I wanted to, but I need to sort out the cramping, which I presume will only go when the sciatica has eased.

Iced the calf when I got back and hopefully no damage done, but we will see in the morning. Booked a physiotherapist session on Monday to see if things can be sorted, but I'm not giving up hope until the last minute, if I can stop the cramping I can do the run!

Been reading other peoples blogs, some running well, some getting injuries, but the support is tremendous, thanks everybody for the positive comments. Two months tomorrow I plan to be lining up at the start of the VLM, I hope my body will let me get there, we shall see. I should have been running around 14-16 miles by now, my furthest is still only 10 and that was a month ago, fingers crossed the sciatica eases over the weekend and the physiotherapist can work some magic?

February 25th - Physiotherapist today....

Not last chance saloon, but pretty close! Seeing physiotherapist this morning to see what can be done about this wretched sciatica and my calf cramping. I remain positive that it can be sorted in time, reading everybody's blogs really makes me want to get out there and run, so it is hard not being able to, but the words of encouragement really help.

The doctor has put me on double strength co-codamol which has really helped in managing the pain, but it is difficult to tell if the pain has eased now as I am usually feeling woozy for most of the day! Woke up feeling as if the cramp may be easing, my calf constantly feels like it is going to cramp at any time, so I'm hoping this is a good sign?

Definitely not giving up hope yet, my leg does feel better, although I know the drugs are keeping it under control, but I have also asked the doctor to organise physiotherapist through the NHS as well as it is getting quite expensive visiting my local Sports Injury Clinic, not to mention the amount of money I have paid out to the chemist lately!

So, update later on this week as I will wait a few days before venturing out again. I would prefer to try a run when it is a bit warmer too as the cold does not help with the cramping at all, but that may be wishful thinking. Carrying on with the stretching and ice/heat treatment as well which seems to help a lot, but it is definitely the sciatica which is causing the tightness in the leg muscles and therefore the cramping.

Everybody has been getting in some really long runs as well lately, great stuff, especially Hollywood Dave who seems to have pushed through the pain barrier for a great run, inspiration to us all!

Good luck with the running everybody, I hope to be back out there with you very soon, I'll keep you all posted.

To: John Adam
Sent: Thu, 28 October, 2010 18:37:04
To: John Adam
Subject: Latest updates

Dear John

Saw the Surgeon today in Bristol. The tumour is still growing into the space he made during the operation and will eventually take away all my functions and put me in a wheelchair, along with more pain of course. The latter they can control but if it gets too much they could take out a bit more of the growing tumour to make me last a bit longer. More radically they have offered to remove the tumour completely and render me paralyzed/paraplegic. Not a cure as the cells are still circulating in the nervous system, but it would likely buy me some more time living, albeit with a different quality of life.

It was at this stage of his illness that Neil began to explore the possibilities of alternatives to the palliative care he was receiving. We talked about removing the tumour completely which would buy him more time, but paralyse him from the waist down. Given that he was now using a catheter this was not such a radical solution, but very scary. It was not a cure however as the cancerous cells would still be in his nervous system and would eventually kill him.

Neil very soon dismissed the idea as at that stage he had no idea of timescale. He was able to maintain a reasonable quality of life and despite the gloomy prognosis he felt reasonably positive about the future. How he managed to maintain such a positive outlook to his condition I have no idea, but he steadfastly refused to give into his condition.

9 SITUATION NOT GOOD

March 6th - Still hoping, still not running.

Went for a run last Wednesday two days after physiotherapist and cramped after half a mile. With no blood getting to my calf muscle due to the sciatica this will always happen, so I have to wait until the sciatica eases. I am keeping fit by walking and cycling and hoping that my core fitness will stand me in good stead if I can get some running in before the big day.

I have been referred for physiotherapist on the NHS as it was getting mighty expensive and was seen yesterday. The good news is they can see no reason why I can't run the marathon, the sciatica should have eased enough by then, so fingers crossed I can still make it. I put my chances at around 70/30 which is way better than a week ago.

I have a lot of exercises to do every day, but feel I am making progress even though I have not done any meaningful runs in over six weeks now. If the sciatica does ease then I am in business, but will be running at a much slower pace than I was in training for. I was hoping for around 4 hours, but would be happy if I managed it in 5 hours now, maybe even 6 if I can't do much training beforehand, we shall see, but a finish is a finish whatever the time and I have a good reason.

Fund raising has not gone so well as I had all but written off my chances so I have not made much of an effort. If I am to run then I am hoping people who have promised to sponsor me will do so and the amount will creep up. I have a bond place with Cancer Research UK, but I am not sure if £2000 is a target I must reach or I must try to reach? Worried they may ask me to make up the difference if I fall short!

Anyway, that is another problem; today is exercising, staying fit as I can and stretching the tightness in my back and leg. Still hoping.............

March 17th - Time running out?

It has been an interesting week to say the least! Not happy with the NHS physiotherapist I decided to see a recommended osteopath on Tuesday as I am in constant pain from the sciatica. When walking I feel such an urge to break into a run having not run for so long, but as soon as I start to lightly jog the cramp starts, so frustrating. I see people out every day running and it really gets to me, but, it is what it is, I can't run, yet!

So I visited the osteopath on Thursday and to be honest I wasn't expecting much. However, they have given me some hope and I can feel a difference, though whether that means I will be able to run this year I really don't know. I have not trained at all for 8 weeks now and feel that a proper run is now way beyond me. If I can get fixed in time then a light jog/stroll is possible, but would I want that, I don't know. My fundraising has stalled due to my inability to know exactly what the picture is and my fitness level has dropped considerably.

So, I have another appointment on Tuesday and we will see how things go, but I can feel an improvement? I have been told that acupuncture may help as well to ease the trapped nerve. I have obviously been compensating for the dodgy knee in my running and so I have been advised to get the op out of the way, sort out my sciatica and resume training later in the year having deferred my place to 2014.

I must admit I am torn, I so want to run this year for obvious reasons, not least of which is 4 months solid training behind me! However, realistically it makes sense to sort out all these problems and come back fully fit, and wiser, next year.

As well as all these issues I have found out the hotel I booked the night before this year's VLM is non-refundable so I will have wasted 160 pounds! I am really annoyed about this too and have complained, but they refuse to budge which I think is appalling. Surely there is some legislation from the sale of goods act to cover this; I booked through Expedia who have been less than helpful.

At this point though I have not deferred my place and this next week is crucial, but if I have to I really don't want to spend the night in a hotel, which was booked because it was not far from the start, knowing that I won't be running. That would be most upsetting, but I also don't want to let the room go and waste 160 pounds!

So, that is where I am at the moment and from reading the blogs there does seem to be an awful lot of injuries people have picked up. If, and it is a big if at this stage, I manage to sort out this sciatica and get back to running without cramping then I am of the mind I should run slowly round and enjoy the day. I will need to assess my fitness first however and see, but if I am able to jog slowly then I think I would be okay to make it run in around 6 hours? Not the 4 hours I was aiming for, but then again I am doing it for Cancer Research UK and my brother, not for me so I would be happy to just finish. If my sciatica proves to be a long term recovery process then it looks like deferral followed by a knee op, rehabilitation and a return to full time training again around October time.

Great to read everybody's blogs and see how well some of you are doing, Hollywood is doing a great job and must be the most positive person ever, hope he manages to get himself back to some sort of fitness, he deserves it! Good running everybody.

March 23rd - Decision time soon?

So physiotherapist went well and I walked better for a while, but then I started to feel really bad, headaches, stomach ache and a general feeling of had enough? I decided it was the co-codamol and stopped taking them, within two days I felt much better, but the downside was the sciatica which has been awful. So it is feeling generally bad, but with no intense pain running down my leg from hip to shin or feel fine and put up with excruciating spasms of pain? I must admit I was at a very low ebb today and had some very negative feelings; I eventually succumbed and took a couple of co-codamol which took the edge off the shooting spasms up and down my leg. Now sat typing with a glass of wine to anesthetize myself!

My race number arrived today as well, talk about mixed feelings opening that envelope! Still, I should think myself lucky, I'm still here, still able to get about and despite the constant pain, managing to hold down a job. Reading some of the blogs can be hard, but respect to Hollywood and Vin who are also struggling with injuries at the wrong time, hoping they make it, both deserve to through sheer bloody-mindedness!

I think I may cancel the physiotherapist on Tuesday though as at £40:00 a go it has had no effect and I know every exercise and stretch I need to do, every one of which is very painful and seems to have no effect as well? I need an injection of a strong painkiller or muscle relaxant straight into my right buttock!!! What I would give to be pain free at the moment......

Anyway, options are, carry my place over to next year and, hopefully, be rid of the damn sciatica and train carefully after an op on my left knee to repair the torn cartilage. Or, try a gentle jog this week to see where I am as regards fitness and cramping of the right calf. If I don't cramp I may ease back to running further over the next few weeks and see how that goes, but if I do cramp it is a deferral to 2014 and watch from the side-lines to cheer the rest of you on.

Keep you posted, but good luck to everybody for your last long runs and tapering, but especially to those of you who, like me, are really struggling with injuries

March 25th - Deferred until 2014

It's been a hard decision, but one which was out of my hands eventually, I have decided to defer until next year and made the phone call this morning. I was surprised by how upset I was, four months of training and then two months of fighting an injury, it has been an emotional rollercoaster!

So now I have to look at getting back to fitness and starting all over again in the autumn, though I shall start running again as soon as I am able to. The sciatica is still bad and that needs to go before I can do any running, but cycling and walking are fine. There is the small matter of the cartilage tear and the operation I need, but once that is done and rehabilitation is sorted then I should be able to run freely and without injury.

I am gutted if I am honest, I was really looking forward to running in April and reading all the blogs has been incredibly inspiring, everybody on their own journey towards one common goal, it feels like an exclusive club that no one else understands? Thanks to everybody for all your support, words of wisdom etc., it has all been appreciated and I wish you all the best of luck with the rest of your training, but especially the big day. I will be with you in spirit if not in person.

One final note, it looks like I may not be able to use the hotel I booked many months ago due to my imminent knee op now. It is the Mercure near Greenwich Park, ideal for the start of the VLM. It is transferable, so if anybody is interested in a room for the night before the run please get in contact. It is paid for already £160.00, so if you are interested you would just need to pay me and I can transfer the room over to your name. Any reasonable offers accepted as you would be doing me a favour!

Happy running everybody, onwards and upwards as Hollywood would say!

From: Neil Adam
Sent: Sun, 21 November, 2010 11:31:53
Subject: Mobility issues

Hi John

I have been in touch with my GP re the worsening situation with my legs, which in the past few days has been rapid. As the situation stands tonight I cannot get down the stairs standing up, I have to come down sitting on the stairs. Once downstairs I am confined to a bed in the lounge and the toilet is down a step in another room.

I need some practical help with wheelchair access, ramps etc. and perhaps getting my mobility scooter into the house rather than the garage. Pain in the back is manageable with 70mg of slow release morphine twice a day so although I am trying to remain positive I am scared that this situation has quickly become unsafe and worrying given the events of just the last few days. We cannot cope with this at home on our own now with the facilities we currently have.

Never one to sit still, he was unfortunately beginning to have some mobility issues; he had already fallen over a few times and had long since given up driving, but in one horrible week he completely lost the use of his legs and found himself requiring the use of a wheelchair.

This was a major change and happened incredibly quickly considering he was reasonably mobile after the last operation. It had a huge impact on his day to day living arrangements as now he was unable to get up and down the stairs or indeed anywhere without assistance.

A bed was set up in the lounge and that became a bedroom with items that he needed close to hand, but this was yet another change in his lifestyle that he had to come to terms with, not easy when you have been an active individual.

10 A CHANGE OF FOCUS

April 10th - Onwards and Upwards!

To use a well-known quote from Hollywood! Not blogged for a while, but I have been reading the fantastic stories on here every day as you all taper off for the 21st. Can't deny that I am gutted inside about not being able to run, but look forward to getting myself back to full fitness and on the road again to 2014. So, onwards and upwards it is with mixed feelings for this year's race, but hoping that Hollywood, Vin et al will have a great run after all the problems people have had to date.

It really is an incredible journey that we all embark on and inevitably, as in all walks of life, there will be some who fall by the wayside. Unfortunately one of those is me, but I am constantly lifted by the wonderful stories on here and the incredible camaraderie and support.

On the home front, I am still in some pain from the sciatica, but it is fading slightly and hopefully it will disappear very soon. I may try jogging lightly as well, but don't want to bring back the dreaded cramping! However, jogging may be off the menu for a while as I saw my consultant last week and my operation on my knee to repair the tear I have will be within the next two months. Out the same day, crutches for a few days and then rehabilitation leading to gentle exercise and hopefully back running again as soon as I can.

The weather is picking up at last, the 21st promises to be a great day for you all and I will be cheering you all on, especially Hollywood and Vin who have been an inspiration to us all. I am going to keep this blog going right the way through to VLM 2014 so I will post the details of my rehabilitation and my own journey. I never forget that "Running for Neil" was started because I wanted to complete the London Marathon in honour of my brother who lost his battle with cancer early last year and to raise money for Cancer Research UK. Good running everybody, take it easy before the big day, I wish you all the best!

April 19th - Good Luck Everybody!

I started my blog way back in October after receiving the news that I had a place in the VLM as a way of documenting my journey towards completing one of the greatest races in the World in honour of my brother Neil. It soon became a diary of the highs and lows of training. No one can understand the strength of character that is needed to push your body further than it has ever gone before, each session working towards running 26.2 miles.

Only I quickly found out that there are people who do understand quite well, those of you who are also making this journey and were documenting your own highs and lows. Making the occasional entry about my latest run I began to read other blogs and soon it became an integral part of my routine. Many hours have been spent reading other people's training issues and what a joy it has been to share the same experiences. Slowly a sort of community of running pals emerged and became a part of my life. The determination of various people like Vin and Hollywood together with the many comments of encouragement has been a highlight of my day now for many months.

Getting badly injured myself, I have been appreciative of the support I have been given and now that the day is nearly here, although I am sad not to be able to run, it feels that I am involved purely because of Real Buzz. My journey continues, training for 2014 will hopefully start again in October and I will continue to document my training highs and lows through to next year.

So thanks guys for all your messages over the last few months, I have really enjoyed reading your blogs and wish you all the best on Sunday, I will be cheering you on and hoping that you all make it safely to the end.

April 22nd - Well done everybody!

Watched as much of the race as I could and all the build-up, then started to read the blogs, anxiously waiting for those who have had injury problems to see if they made it. Incredible stories of will and determination, sheer guts on the part of many. It looked to be an awesome day and I am even more determined to run it next year. I have my place already having deferred due to injury so I have booked my hotel! This time I intend to be there, so training will be slow and steady as soon as my op is out the way and I can get back to full fitness.

Inspired by all the incredible stories on Real Buzz and feeling the sciatica much less now I decided to get on my bike tonight to see how it felt. So at 7:30, having cleaned, oiled and generally serviced a bike that I haven't been on since my back went way back at the end of January, I set off. It felt great, no twinges from my back, legs were fine and it was good to be exercising again. Tomorrow I will start riding to work again and keep that up until my knee operation.

Today is now the beginning of my training for VLM 14 - Onwards and Upwards (now where have I heard that before?)

April 29th - Ballot Entry

A week since the VLM and I've enjoyed reading everyone's posts. Incredible tales of determination and triumph, it has increased my desire to run this amazing race next year. Although I already have a place through Cancer Research I decided to go for a ballot entry as it takes the pressure off the fundraising part. I am sure I will raise more money as the year progresses, but if I get a ballot place it will make it easier to concentrate on the training. If I don't then I'm still in and will need to start an early push to raise funds.

I still have sciatica, but it is much better and I cycled to work all last week as well as walking. Not tried running yet as I think it best to try that after my knee operation as that will give the sciatica more time to go. It has eased considerably, so I am hoping I am at the end as it was very painful for months and I thought it would never go.

Feel very positive about next year, so positive in fact that I have already booked my hotel! Knowing I already have a place let me book early which was at least half the price of the last time I booked for this year. They really do bump the prices up around that weekend, but I guess that is business.

Waiting to hear about my knee op is a bit disheartening as it has been 4 weeks since I saw the surgeon who had indicated a waiting time of 4 to 8 weeks, so I'm expecting to hear any time now. The wait is annoying though; I have got time off work when I need it and for the recovery, but will be back into work on crutches as soon as I can. I desperately want to get back to training again, so everything is on hold at the moment which is more frustrating than not being able to run the VLM this year.

I almost booked the Great South Run, but as it is in October I don't want to push just yet in case there is a problem with my knee, but if all goes well I will enter as soon as I feel able to run it. I think this year I will enter a few more races to get a better feel for running in crowds; many of you posted how it was sometimes difficult to run with any kind of rhythm due to the large amount of runners.

So ballot entered, exercise started again, hotel booked and knee op imminent, things are beginning to slot into place, albeit slowly, but I do intend to take the training a little more seriously this time and not force the miles. Running for my brother has inspired me in many ways and as many of you have noted, Sunday was not the end of the journey but the beginning. Happy running everybody!

From: Neil Adam
Sent: 09/12/2010 22:57 GMT
To: John Adam
Subject: Mobility Scooter

Hi John,

It was great to get on the scooter when you were here, Mobility has called back several times asking for dimensions, they think they have a nearly new van sized to take the scooter and wheelchair, will know more tomorrow. But I still worry about how to get onto the scooter? I am like a sack of meat, the surgeon suggests that nothing is reversible on this and the legs, maybe a possibility it could affect the arms too. So stuff from your worst nightmares, I wake up in the night sweating from running and swimming sometimes too. Then the darkness and the pain hit me. I wonder how dad would have coped with this disease.

Neil busied himself with organising a mobility scooter and obviously, being a confirmed petrol head, he researched the best model he could and pretty soon he was whizzing around the roads where he lived. This gave him a renewed passion that was noticeable every time I visited and with the pain under control he was more his usual self.

He had completely lost the use of his legs by now so getting on and off the scooter was not the easiest of tasks, but once he was on it was obvious to all how much he enjoyed the freedom to get out in the fresh air. I remember him saying to me at the time how much more you appreciate the simple things in life when faced with adversity.

Despite the positive attitude during the day Neil experienced dreams of life as it was that left him distressed when he woke up. Impossible to understand how that must of felt, but it was comforting to hear him speak of our father. Dad was not a good patient at all, in fact he hated hospitals and never visited the doctor. There was no way that dad would have coped with such a serious illness and in some ways he was lucky to have dropped dead from an aneurysm. Much as it was a shock to the family, we all agreed that for him, that was the best way to go.

11 INTO THE UNKNOWN

May 12th - Improving slowly.

I read a lot of the other posts on here every day and it is beginning to become a bit of a routine. From the crazy races some of you have entered through to the more traditional events around the country. It seems that we all have running bug and it is difficult to stop once you start, short of injury that is.

Been cycling back and forth to work for a while now and certainly the legs have got much stronger. I still have twinges from the Sciatica and my left knee is very sore, but I work through those small irritations. I now have a date for my knee op; pencilled in for the 25th of June, later than I would have hoped for and being the NHS I'm not holding my breath. I might be lucky with a cancellation and they will push me further up the list or there is always the possibility of my op being cancelled as well.

Still, I had a letter from the consultant asking me to confirm I still wanted the operation. After four years of knee pain I think I might still want the procedure!

Despite the cycling though I am putting on weight and am desperately missing the running. I had decided I would not run anymore until after my knee was sorted and I could run without pain, but as the sciatica has improved I am considering going for a short run pre-op. I like Vin's plan, a steady 2 miles until it becomes routine and then upping the pace for speed work. I could use that plan when I get back to proper running later on in the year, but for now, a steady run for two miles would be a good start.

Happy running everybody.

May 19th - Hey Shorty, it's your Birthday!

How did that happen? Another year gone and now I find myself sitting here wondering how I should feel at 56! Goals? I intended to run the London Marathon before I was 50, but things got in the way! Intended to run it aged 55, but injuries put a stop to that too!

Positives? I jumped out of bed this morning with no back pain, first time for a long time. My operation has been brought forward to June 3rd, so I have a week off for half term followed by the op on the Monday and possibly another week convalescing at home. Fortunately it is not a difficult week at work so they will be able to cover me easily enough. As soon as I can I will get back to work, crutches or not and take it easy at my desk.

Friends who have had the operation tell me they were off crutches after two or three days and exercising lightly fairly quickly. I am hoping that this will allow me to run without that burning sensation in my left knee and a constant soreness. Time will tell.

So, 56! Don't feel it, probably look it, but age is just a number, I feel good this morning. When I got to 50 I bought myself an electric drum kit so this morning I've enjoyed drumming away to ZZ Top and Genesis. (I have an eclectic taste in music!) Even tried 'Double Bass Drum' which is really hard on the legs, but great excrcise.

All in all I feel pretty good and looking forward to a meal out with the family. Still enjoying reading the posts on here, Hollywood's adventure in mud looked absolutely insane and I'm hoping I can enter a few races before VLM 2014. Happy Running everybody.

From: Neil Adam
To: John Adam
Sent: 31:12:2010
Subject: New Van

Happy New Year Bruv, we are having a quiet night, both kids are back at some time. Had the Mercedes demo today, fantastic motor, it can take the scooter, wheelchair, commode and 3 people; it has a power lift and auto gears and doors. Linda drove it to Bisley and seems up for driving it, it's a 2 litre Diesel. Mods required to lift and other bits so will be ready by mid Jan. £46 a week to hire including insurance! Nice motor, hope I can drive it in future if I can get off these anti fit pills, which is a possibility after I spoke to the doctor today. Steroids reduced today and I feel well. Hope for period of stability now?

 As well as the mobility scooter Neil was interested in getting hold of a van which would make it easier for him to get out and about. The medication he was on had given him hope that he would live a lot longer and he remained positive about his situation. Obviously he continued to plan and research every detail of his life which was important for his state of mind as it gave him an interest.

Getting hold of a suitable mode of transport gave him a focus, something to look forward to as he was pretty much confined to the area around his village. By this time the first scooter had been replaced by a more robust electronic wheelchair which made it easier for him to move around the house and get out and about. This would also lock into the van and increase his freedom to visit various places instead of being stuck in the village where he lived.

12 AT THE MERCY OF THE NHS

June 2nd - Operation time.......

So the day has finally arrived, well nearly! Had my pre-op assessment on Wednesday and I'm good to go, being dropped off by my wife at 7.00am tomorrow morning and then it's into the hospital gown and wait until called. General anaesthetic, so asleep whilst the surgeon does his stuff. Two, maybe three incisions and then hopefully he will trim the torn cartilage and give the knee a good clean out. I should be ready for collection by the afternoon and then its leg up for 48 hours and rest until the end of the week.

The French Open is in the second week, so I may glance at that, but I have got some work to do as well. As long as I'm not in any discomfort I should be able to get on with stuff. I can see the tennis being a distraction though, shame!

I am hoping that this will be the beginning of my journey towards VLM 2014. Hopefully the knee will improve so I can run again and with the Sciatica getting better every day I should be able to start training again. If all goes well I may enter the Great South Run, time will tell. Happy running everybody!

June 3rd - Knee operation went okay.

So back at home after arthroscopic surgery on my knee and now back at home resting up and waiting for the drugs to wear off. My wife dropped me off just before 7:00am and after checking in I settled down to wait, but I didn't have to wait long and I can't praise the NHS enough as I was treated superbly from arriving to leaving.

After a short wait I was called through to carry out a number of pre-op procedures and then before long I had to get changed into the dreaded gown and wait with a couple of other guys in the waiting room before theatre. Interesting guys to talk to, always fascinating to hear other people's stories and how they got there?

Then it was up to theatre and whilst waiting for the anaesthetist some guy to the left of me asks me if I taught at his old school years back? Turns out I taught him 30 years ago when I started teaching in Portsmouth! After 35 years of teaching I don't get recognised that much, but it is always nice when you do.........sometimes!

Then it was into theatre and before I knew it I was out for the count. After many strange dreams I was awoken by a lovely nurse with a drink of water and as she slowly brought me round the surgeon visited me to let me know what he had done, trimmed the small tear on my cartilage and cleaned out the knee joint, some signs of early arthritis, but all went well.

I was transferred to a side ward, given a cup of tea and toast after dressing and then pottered down to the car park where my wife drove me home. I'm on crutches, but feel okay to weight bear, just a bit woozy, or I was as I've had a sleep and just feel sore around the knee now, may need some painkillers soon.

I feel okay, bit sick I suppose and obviously the knee area is sore, but otherwise the whole experience was very good, so as I say, the NHS can take a bow as far as I'm concerned. (Still don't understand the many people who look at deaths door sitting outside the hospital smoking, they are invariably obese and quite young, no wonder the NHS is stretched, people don't help themselves do they, get running I say!)

So there it is, recuperation under way, lovely weather, tennis on the TV and signed off for at least a week, happy days and not long until that first run. Thank you everybody for your kind words, I will be reading and commenting on various blogs over the next few days, it always makes for fascinating reading, Real Buzzers are a breed apart!

Happy Running everybody!

June 8th - Post Operation - knee feels okay and there's a bonus.......

So five days after my knee operation and I feel okay, so far anyway! Went for a short walk today with my wife, bit tight around the knee, but no pain and fine when I got back. Do my exercises every day and everything seems to be working okay. I have had my leg up in the garden every day this week, took the whole week off work eventually, I have been signed off for two weeks, but I'm going back on Monday as the knee is fine and there is very little swelling. Stitches come out in a week and I'm going to venture out for a short jog.

The bonus is, the sciatica seems to have gone, no sign of it and I can only conclude that under a general anaesthetic my body relaxed so much the trapped nerve in my back released itself finally. I have no pain in my lower back, no pain running down my leg and no pain around my right hip. I can't remember the last time I didn't have any pain from the sciatica, so

I'm really pleased. I am doing back exercises as well to make sure I don't get a recurrence of the problems I had.

As soon as my knee feels strong enough it will be back to training which I'm really looking forward to, although with some trepidation obviously. I am going to take it steady, there is plenty of time, but I feel so much better and ready to test the knee out. I'm off the drugs as well, so able to have a beer, cheers!

June 17th - The road to recovery starts here!

Stitches came out today, remarkably painless too, I expected some discomfort but felt nothing. Today is therefore the first day of my road to recovery which should end at VLM 2014. As Vin has noticed, the fitness leaves you very quickly so it will be a long, long road I reckon!

My knee feels good, difficult to distinguish between the soreness post-op and pre-op apart from the position of it. It won't be until I try running that I will be able to assess if it has been a success I guess?

Anyway, the plan is to walk for the rest of this month as I think jogging is pushing it too early, so I'm going to walk every day and build up my leg strength slowly. I strapped my knee this evening and then set off on my 3 mile route hoping to do a mile at least. I also set my Garmin as I'm going to record this journey right the way through to the start line of the London Marathon. Set off at a brisk pace, turned out to be around 15 min mile pace which made me laugh a bit as I was recording 8:30 - 9:00 min miles before I got injured!

That pace was okay though and I covered a mile in just under 15 minutes and felt okay, so I kept going until I felt a few twinges and eased back to finish at 1.5 miles in 22 minutes and 5 seconds. The knee feels a bit sore, but nothing bad at all and an hour later I've not had a reaction at all. The real test will be a jog, but even though I desperately want to run again I know I need to take this slowly, but I can see what Hollywood Dave goes on about, it's the challenge of it and once you've got the bug you want to beat it, you have to beat it or you can't rest. I dream of running nowadays and I know I won't be truly happy until I can start pounding the streets again and then it won't be just getting running again, it will be running at a quicker pace than last time, then running further than last time, then running faster and further than last time!

Can you tell that I want to get out there again? Glad to see that people are starting to recover from their injuries and are getting back out there, I'm not sure how fit I will be by the time of the Real Buzz run in September, it may come too soon for me, but I am keeping an open mind. I want to run the Great South Run, but that is only a possibility at the moment. I am on the road to recovery at last and intend to take it steady, but I will be on the start line in April, happy running everybody.

June 30th - Taking it easy, Vin Style!

Great to read that Vin managed his Park Run, something I will be aiming for at some stage. He has shown me the way however, take it slow, take it steady and listen to your body. It's nearly 4 weeks since my op and I've managed the knee carefully, I was keen to run as soon as I could, but after reading up a bit more about the operation I have reconsidered any ideas of running yet.

I don't want to undo any good done by the surgeon, so I am walking when I can and cycling to work, although I only have a week left and then eight weeks holiday!   I will start light jogging on grass, like Vin, when I feel I can manage it and build from there. At the moment the knee is sore and I feel quite frustrated that the healing process is taking longer than I thought, but it is what it is and I have 9 months to get ready. As Vin said, no silly injuries this time, take it slow and steady and build up sensibly, increasing distance and pace when it feels right and easing back when I need to.

Feeling slightly negative at the moment as the sciatica has returned, though not as bad thank goodness, but it is there still and I am a bit despondent about not running since the end of January, but the Real Buzzers keep spirits up, everybody has some problems at some stage, the support keeps you plodding on.

So, hoping to get a long walk in this week, knee still strapped, and see what the reaction is, long term aim run/jog in another two weeks on grass for a mile, walking if needed. Park Run as soon as I feel I'm ready for it, not before! Enjoy the weather everybody, good running.

From: Neil Adam
To: John Adam
Sent: Sun, 10 February, 2011 1
Subject: Getting around

Hi John,

We have been out in the Van every day since Sunday....we do get around! I am suffering a bad breakdown of the skin around my hips and it has to be dressed every day, with an hour lying on my side after the Carers have gone at 9 am. I have also developed sores which looks a bit raw, so I have to have some special cream for that now. So what with my injection every day it's usually about 11 to 11.30 before we can get out. But I am fighting on despite all these extra burdens. The only positive is that I can feel nothing down there, and I am getting no tumour pain with the drug regime I am on.

The Mercedes van made a huge difference to his life allowing Linda to drive him around to places for visits, whether it was for medical reasons or for pleasure. There were more phone calls from Neil as he called me from the various places they went to and he seemed much happier. This positive attitude was never more obvious during this period and gave us all hope that maybe, just maybe, the tumour would stop growing and he could have a period of stability in his health.

He still had issues obviously, mostly associated with spending a lot of time sitting or lying and every day he went through a grueling routine to get him up and ready. I never once heard him complain, indeed he usually greeted me with one of his awful jokes. It was good to see him in such good spirits and I usually timed my visits to arrive just as was ready for the day. His determination to live every day to the best of his ability given the obstacles he faced was inspirational to say the least.

13 RECOVERY CONTINUES

July 8th - First run after the op!

Feeling inspired by Andy Murray's brilliant win yesterday and also Vin's Park Run I decided to give it a go and see where I was regarding my recovery. So, compression stocking on, running socks, Rock Tape on the knee, Garmin on my wrist and headphones on I set off slowly walking my usual 5K. Feeling okay I started to jog lightly and carried on until my knee started to feel sore so I eased back to walking.

Set myself a target and started running again going further this time and then walking again. Set myself a target again and ran a bit further this time, settling into a reasonable pace and feeling okay, but as the familiar feelings came back and I settled into a comfortable pace I realised that in listening out for any problems with my knee I was less aware of how unfit I had become, until I felt most uncomfortable and had to stop, but not because of my knee this time!

My ankles were also not used to running and complained a bit, but the knee held out okay for two miles at around 11:30 pace which is not too bad for my start back to fitness after my injury problems. I feel much more positive after that run, my first run in nearly six months so it is definitely onwards and upwards from here which means I should be fine for the run on the 8th September wherever that will be.

Take it easy running in this weather, so warm.

July 30th - Je suis en France!

Hence no blogging for quite a while, but now on a site where there is Internet access and sat in the shade enjoying the views across the French countryside. Tried to catch up with a few blogs, impressed by the progress Vin has made and hoping HD gets his mojo back for his latest challenge. Hoping to read a few more in the coming days.

Brought my running gear with me with the intention of trying a few runs, but the heat, 34 degrees, have meant I have not been able to get out at all and if I'm honest it is because I'm not 100% sure about my knee yet. Saw my surgeon before I set off to France and he is happy with everything, but told me to be patient, the site where the camera was inserted during the op is a bit sore still, but the whole area still feels tight and I can't yet bend the knee properly.

So I am continuing with the stretching exercises and walking as much as I can in this heat.

Whenever I feel a bit dispirited I think about some of the challenges many of you have faced and overcome and know that I just need to take it steady and let my body know when it is ready to resume training. It is not going as well as I thought it would, but I have noticed some improvement in both the knee and my sciatica. I hope to do a lot more walking when I get back as I have heard that can really improve my back problem and therefore ease the sciatica.

My aim is a 5k run in under 30 minutes by the end of August which I think is achievable. I have managed a couple of short runs easily enough, but I haven't run consistently at a steady pace yet and that is what I need to.

Good running everyone.

From: Neil Adam
To: John Adam
Sent: Sun, 20 February, 2011 18:23:01
Subject: Hospital again

Dear John

Since you came to visit last week I unfortunately had a hospital visit on Friday after I developed chest pains again, this time caused by an inflamed lung which is being treated with antibiotics and painkillers. Not that long ago I would have thought it was a nightmare. How your attitude can change and determine what makes you focus on what's really important to you, in the quality of life and staying alive. The price of gherkins in Turkey seems a long way away now.

Around this time Neil had a few issues that necessitated a few trips to the hospital and there were times when I came to visit that I had to go to the Frenchay hospital in Bristol instead of his house. The episode with his chest pains was quite a frightening time, especially for Linda, but Neil handled it all calmly. His illness had given him a new perspective on life and so he dealt with the problem knowing he was in good hands.

Visiting him in hospital was one of my least favourite times as having spent many hours visiting our mother during the last months of her life it brought back many unhappy memories. Neil was often very sleepy during these visits as well which meant conversation was minimal. I was also often ushered out whilst various procedures were carried out, but despite all this I was always pleased to see him.

14 THE LONG ROAD BACK.

August 16th - First 5K since my knee operation!

Apologies for not keeping up to date with everybody's blogging whilst I've been away, I managed to post once in France, but I've been feeling a bit despondent post op as I couldn't see when I was going to be able to run again. The knee has been slow to recover, no pain at all, just discomfort, soreness and tight. The Sciatica has also been a pain, literally, so stretching has been important. This has meant I have not been able to get back to training as quickly as I wanted to so as I mentioned before I did no running on holiday but lots of walking which does help. Had three fantastic (and hot) weeks in France, but put on a bit of weight and so decided to join the local gym to use the facilities I could and get back on track.

I joined on Monday and have been every day since to walk steadily on the running machines and use the elliptical joggers to work up a sweat. Tried jogging lightly on Tuesday, but knee felt a bit tight, so slowed to a fast walk followed by a quick swim, steam room and felt better for exercising. Today I felt a jog might be possible, as my knee felt good and the sciatica had responded to stretching so off I went. I wore my compression socks and strapped the knee and then warmed up on the treadmill before starting to jog steadily and as the knee seemed okay I maintained a steady pace for 10 minutes and then set myself 2 minute goals. Before I knew it I had run for 20 minutes and another 10 seemed possible. There were a few twinges around 28 minutes, but they eased and I finished the run in just a shade under 30 minutes.

Well 3 miles actually, but even so I'm really pleased to finally get back to running albeit on the dreaded treadmill. 3 miles in 30 minutes though and although it wasn't easy, it wasn't that bad, the knee was fine, but I was knackered at the end, so very unfit after nearly six months since I first got injured.

I feel good now, though watching Mo Farah probably helped, incredible running! So it's a rest this weekend and then back to light jogging again next week, but I shall not be doing another 5K for a while although my goal is a 5K run on the roads. With the Real Buzz run coming up on the September 8th I am conscious of the fact that it will only be a token effort from me unfortunately, but it's the thought that counts.

I had hoped to get up to one of the events, but at this stage 5K is all I can manage at the moment. So I will donate and run solo on the day and think about all you guys running in the various events around the country for NASS. I hope to organise something orange to wear and put up some photos as well.

VLM London 2014 training has officially started, happy running everybody.

August 23rd - Best 5k time for nearly 2 years!

Feeling pretty chuffed after managing a 5k run on the treadmill in a time of 26 minutes 30 seconds, that's my fastest time for nearly two years and comes after a knee op and a pretty bad case of sciatica. The knee has been getting better and better, though hurting at the front, nowhere near the incisions? Anyway, I thought I might be able to manage a run today so headed off to the gym and after warming up I set off at a reasonable pace making sure I wore a strap on the knee and compression socks. It all seemed to be going quite well, the sciatica doesn't stop me running, it actually helps and after 2k I thought I might be able to wind it up a bit. Although tired I finished strongly and without any knee problems which is a good sign.

It is boring on the treadmill though and I can't wait to get out on the roads, but for now it does me fine, I can stretch, warm up, exercise and then swim and sit in the steam room afterwards and I guess I will be running at the gym when the weather is too bad. Hopefully not as cold as last year though!

Today I played a round of golf, 18 holes, the first time for quite some time, I played well and it was very enjoyable, but my legs ache! Went to the gym to use the cross trainer and then soaked away the aches and pains in the pool.

As I said although the sciatica has been quite painful lately it isn't stopping me running, but I am worried that after nearly 7 months I still have it, albeit not as bad as it was. I stretch every day and that eases it, but every morning I wake up with it and wonder if it will ever go? I have had physiotherapist, sports injury massage, treatment from an osteopath and nothing has really made much difference so I may try the sports therapist at the gym and also go back to the doctor. Still, at least I can run which was not possible when it first appeared as I cramped every time I went out.

So, I'm still in training for VLM 2014 and feeling very positive despite the various niggles I have. Reading other blogs it would seem that many of you are suffering from a few aches and pains at the moment, hopefully everybody will get themselves sorted as Oggie's Real Buzzers run for NASS is coming up very soon. Mental note: I need an orange vest! Take it easy everybody and happy running .

August 26th - Another 5K in the bank, feeling ready for the roads again!

My fitness is improving quite quickly and so I set off to the gym suitably dressed, compression socks, knee strapped and running gear on. Did a series of stretches before warming up, especially a piriformis stretch to help my Sciatica which really helps, but hurts! Then it is a five minute warm up before the 5K. I decided to concentrate on a steady pace this time as I need to build up my stamina again, so settled into a comfortable pace and music on, off I went. As Vin will concur, running on a treadmill is nowhere near as easy as running on the road, but it is what it is and you have to get on with it. I made an effort to run as balanced as I could, I have noticed that I am running much better now my knee has been fixed. I used to protect the bad knee, without realising it obviously, and that was what ultimately put my back out, which then resulted in Sciatica. It is comforting to note the change in my style and obviously this also means I have confidence in the knee.

I finished in just over 28 minutes which was very comfortable and I felt like I could have carried on for a lot longer, but these are early days. My leg muscles were sore, a sure sign of a lack of conditioning as I have run only a few times since my injury way back at the end of January, dark days indeed! However, I feel so much more confident and this time I will train properly for the VLM in April next year and not push the mileage up too quickly.

As for the sciatica, well as I said before, running is a help, though I do notice it when I am running. Thankfully though I don't cramp after a few yards which was why I had to defer my place this year unfortunately.

Like many of you, I guess, I trawl the Internet for solutions to the many problems life throws at you and I have read everything there is on dealing with sciatica and watched too many YouTube videos on stretches to help or cure this painful condition. None seem to work apart from the piriformis stretch which relieves the pain and seems to have a longer term effect. The other day though I found a forum that talked about releasing the muscle through deep tissue massage and it looked interesting. The pain I get, as most people do from this condition, is deep in the buttock and down the thigh to my shin.

I get a lot of relief by massaging the area just below my right hip and slightly in towards the right buttock. This forum suggested you can release the muscle by pushing hard into the area with your thumbs, so I have been giving it a go and boy is it painful! However, it does seem to have an effect as I have been waking up in the morning with far less symptoms than before and even the feeling that it is gone, but I know it isn't yet. Still, it is a relief and I shall keep doing the stretches and the deep massage technique and hopefully the dreaded sciatica will eventually go.

As the title says, I feel ready for the roads again so hopefully next week I will venture out, it is lovely weather for running, enjoy everybody!

August 29th - The Real Buzz spirit.........

Such spirit shines throughout this forum as people often lay their souls bear with tales of adversity that many would shy away from. The advice, inspiration and support that this forum provides is, without doubt, a real positive in what has not always an easy life and in the light of the messages of support I have received lately I thought it prudent to remember why I joined Real Buzz in the first place. Just over three years ago my brother was diagnosed with a spinal cancer so rare only ten cases in the world ever were recorded. It was unfortunately terminal and though he fought bravely and lived longer than he was predicted through sheer bloody-mindedness, he sadly passed away last year. My brother was my only sibling and we were the best of friends, so the loss has been hard to bear. In the months after his death I very much wanted to pay tribute in some way to a man I admired and looked up to all of my life and it was that desire that lead to me signing up for the London Marathon.

As many of you already know, that was cruelly denied me by a knee problem that put my back out and ultimately caused sciatica which meant I had to defer my place to 2014. I was absolutely gutted not to be able to run as it had been such a part of my life, as has Real Buzz. I had joined this forum after a month of training out of curiosity to see what others were doing and maybe get some advice. It very quickly became part of my everyday life and although we have never met I feel I know some of you very well.

My early postings were very much about my runs and how they went, but then the advice started and I moved on to reading other people's posts which were fascinating, inspirational and emotional in equal measure. My posts become more about my feelings than times and distances, although they were still recorded.

As the Real Buzz spirit grew many of you have posted not only about your runs, but also about what was going on in your life and how that had affected you. The various stories leading up to VLM 2013 were incredible and I quickly became part of an online community with a common goal. No need to name names, but some of the posts on here have brought a lump to my throat and a tear to my eye.

During my darkest hours when the sciatica rendered me in so much pain that I did not read or post a great deal the support was amazing. In the lead up to my knee operation and after, again, such was my feeling of desperation about ever running again I did not post very much, but I read others religiously and slowly the enthusiasm began to return. It is infectious and I have never known anything like it. Oggie's run is an amazing feat given that it has all been coordinated by a group of like-minded people that all have a passion for running, yet hardly know each other, incredible and such an honour to be part of.

It would have been very easy to give in to my injury, but I set myself a goal of running the London Marathon to raise money for Cancer Research UK in honour of my brother. It is beyond question that the Real Buzz spirit has kept me positive throughout and I know that I will be on that start line next April and I will finish. Many of you have been incredibly supportive throughout this journey and for that I thank you, I won't name names, you know who you are.

Happy Running everybody and heartfelt thanks.

August 31st - Thanks to Oggie I'm ready for the road!

The timing couldn't have been better really, September 8th is perfect for my first road run since the operation on my knee and after today on the treadmill I feel more than ready. Did my usual 3 miles, but ran at a steady pace, one which is far slower than normal, but I would be comfortable running that speed for VLM 2014. At the moment it is okay, not comfortable yet, but it will be once I increase my fitness.

I run at our gym on a treadmill, which I hate, but it gives you good feedback AND with a mirror in front of you allows you to check your running style. I've noticed I'm running in quite a balanced way now that my knee has been fixed which can only be a good thing and today I was happy jogging along at 9;30 pace which did not challenge me too much. I felt less than comfortable about mid-way through the run, but I evoked the Real Buzz spirit and fought off any negative thoughts and carried onto the end.

What was more pleasing was my pulse rate, it has always been quite low at around 50 bpm, but after running it has been slow to come down. Today it was under a 100 bpm after 2 minutes and in the 70's after 5 minutes. Recovery is as important as warming up, so I am pleased that everything seems to be going in the right direction.

I intend to get on the road this week in preparation for the 8th. I would have liked to have been at an event with other Real Buzzers, but at least I will have my orange NASS shirt on and I will be visible to anybody on my 5K route. It's the taking part that counts and it will be great to think that all around the country there will be runners clad in various orange outfits running for a wonderful cause, brilliant.

So, things are looking good, although it really is about time I got rid of this sciatica which I guess is due to my initial problem with my back. I am looking after my back and stretch everyday as well as exercise, so I don't see why it hasn't gone, any ideas (or cures)?

Anyway, fantastic weather, long may it last, happy running everybody.

From: Neil Adam
To: John Adam
Sent: Thu, 24 March, 2011 20:05:15
Subject: Consultant

Hi John,

Today the consultant told me I have a Palsy on my left side, ear is partly deaf and the eye does not close properly. Also this morning I noticed my mouth was a bit droopy. So she has put me back on Steroids to try and cure it. Also no guarantee it's not caused by the tumour, so may have to have a scan to see if the damn thing has travelled. Another worry.

I began to notice a change in his appearance the last time I had visited, but Neil confirmed by email that he had a palsy on the left side of his face. They were not sure if it was the tumour travelling or something related to the medication he was taking, but he was to have another scan to see what the problem was.

This seemed to be the pattern of things now, just when he had a period of stability something else would crop up to knock him sideways and so would begin tests and procedures and finally more medication. Neil took it all in his stride and continued to plane for activities in the coming months. Such was his positivity that it was difficult to believe that he would die sooner rather than later. Despite all the problems he faced he seemed to deal with them and move on displaying an indomitable spirit that refused to be beaten.

15 MAKING PROGRESS

September 3rd - 5K PB! Best time for 4 years and now ready for Sunday. Had an unbelievable run tonight, albeit on the treadmill, but I managed a 5K in 24 minutes 58 seconds which I am really pleased with. I have not gone under 25 minutes for over 4 years; I never expected to get back under 25 minutes ever again, so this was quite a run. In case anybody is worried about me pushing it, my best ever time for 5K was 22:30 and I used to regularly run under 24 minutes, so 25 minutes used to be an easy run, back in the day.

Since my knee problems I had slowed down, though I still managed to dip under 25 minutes for the Winchester 5K, but that was in 2009 and I haven't got near it since. I never realised how much the knee was affecting my running and I wish I had pushed for the op much sooner, then I wouldn't have put my back out and subsequently have got sciatica.

Still, it is what it is and I am glad to be running fairly pain free and getting back to full fitness, it really feels glorious to be able to run freely and now I have to translate that to the road again. I had a go at a steady 5K on the road this Sunday and it was much harder than the treadmill. Watching the kerb, dodging people, waiting for cars to cross a road and concentrating on a smooth run really sapped the energy, but I did it and now feel ready for Sunday. I want to run at a reasonable, but steady pace as I want to enjoy the run and reflect on what is happening all over the country as Real Buzzers venture out in various orange outfits, should be a great day and although I am running a private 5K I am quite excited to be part of it all and look forward to all blog updates and pictures! Happy running everybody and good luck for Sunday :-)
September 6th - Last run before Sunday and Real Buzzers Great Oggie Run.

It is with mixed emotions I am writing this having read Hollywood Dave's blog. So sorry to hear the problems that he has got and hope that he can face the challenges that lie ahead. Truth be told I know he will face them head on, it's not in his nature to do anything but go forward, but I hope that he gets his problems sorted. He has been such an inspiration to me throughout all my problems that there is no question of me reciprocating, you can't keep a great man down!

On a positive note, I ran a steady 3 miler today at the gym on the dreaded treadmill and settled for a nice easy pace. I finished in 28 minutes and felt good, not struggling for breath, knee was fine; sciatica didn't bother me at all so all good. Finding myself comfortable at a 9 min pace and now need to work towards strength in my legs so that I can move up from 3 miles.

I am in no hurry though as I am beginning to enjoy running free of pain, it is wonderful to be able to just get lost in the moment. It's been a long time since I was able to do that and it feels good.

My running vest from NASS arrived today thank goodness, I was beginning to get worried, it's a bit small, but okay for Sunday. I never know what to order as Large and Extra Large can be so different. My Extra Large shirt from Cancer Research UK was way too big, so I went for a Large for my NASS shirt and it is quite a small Large! Never mind, it will be fine on the day and more than suitable for some pictures as well.
Anyway, feel fine for Sunday and look forward to it, but thinking of HD and hoping all goes well. Good luck everybody for Sunday!

September 8th - Painting the town Orange.......

Well not quite, but I had my NASS orange vest on and I ran round the local roads! Anyway, woke up excited about my run today for many reasons, but mostly because I knew that many of you would be getting ready for various events around the UK and running clad mostly in orange for Oggie's run and NASS.

I tried to treat it like an event run, so I got up early and had some porridge, then took it easy and stretched out gently before donning the orange NASS vest and putting on my usual running kit. Got my wife to take a picture of me, which generally I hate, but I was proud to wear the vest so did not complain.

The forecast was grim, but the sun was out, so after setting my Garmin off I went on my usual route. I wanted to take it steady and enjoy the run, but I am conscious of the fact that I am back in training for VLM 2014. I started off at a reasonable pace, listening to my iPod and enjoying the many glances I got regarding the bright orange vest! I felt good, knee was fine, no niggles and then at 1 mile the heavens opened and I got drenched! I loved it, it put a smile on my face as I ploughed on absolutely soaking wet and at 2 miles I felt very comfortable in my running at least.

I was now running around the 9 min per mile pace and although faster than last time I ran on the road, it wasn't a problem, but I slowed down anyway as I felt I could go on longer if I wanted to. Could I have run further today, certainly, could I have run a half marathon, probably not, but I am improving week on week and with 7 months to go feel much more confident.

As I ran I thought of Hollywood and hoped that he was okay and also of all you other Real Buzzers out running for Oggie and NASS. I really enjoyed the run, which considering it was only my second time out on the roads since my operation is a real boost for me. My route is shown below and is one I use to gauge my fitness, just 3 miles or 5K really.

The end of the run seemed to come all too quickly, which is a good thing as I wasn't labouring at all and at that point the sun emerged and I began to dry as I warmed down and made my way home. I felt good, pleased with my run and honoured to be a part of a very special day. The stats below from my Garmin tell the story of my run, short it may be, but it means I am going in the right direction, albeit slowly. This time I intend to make the start line in April.

So, that's my story, looking forward to reading about everybody else's runs today, there are sure to be some fantastic pictures and tales!
I took a picture just after I finished and I think it sums up my run perfectly!
Hope the day went well for everybody.

September 13th - Real Buzz support is second to none!

I will be honest, I was feeling a few twinges from my knee which worried me and I was also feeling a bit under the weather. So today's run was looking increasingly unlikely much as I needed to run. Then I logged on to RB and saw Vin's reply, Jim's dare and Oggie's comment which raised the spirits somewhat. Read a few more blogs, including the excellent blog by BB and then packed my kit and off I went. It's amazing what a few well-chosen words can do, so buoyed by the RB spirit I ran my usual 5K in 27 minutes on the dreaded treadmill.

This was my second 5K run this week; I did 26 minutes on Tuesday after Sunday's 28 minutes on the road. I am keeping to 5K about 3 times a week and aiming to get comfortable at 9 min a mile pace. I hope to be able to run the VLM at that pace and aim to get round in 4 hours or so. I am not going to be silly with my training, there is plenty of time and I need to get some conditioning back in my legs and feel comfortable in my running style. As I'm no longer protecting the knee it is a case of improving my fitness slowly and knowing that I can run on from 5K with no problems at the same pace.

I will start a conservative marathon plan as soon as I feel comfortable on

my runs and move the mileage up, but slowly this time. Last year I went from 3 miles to 6 miles to 10 miles too quickly and in a short space of time. I will also do some speed training with intervals at least once a week, plus there is my cycling, walking and my back exercises!
I reckon I should be able to stay healthy and fit as long as I am sensible and listen to my body, last year I thought it was a given I would be on that start line, now I know better.

Loving the Oggie's run stories, what a great day everybody had and I hope to meet up with some of you guys at the VLM 2014 start line. I also hope that all goes well for the one in a million guy known as Hollywood Dave. He has a mountain to climb but I know we will all be behind him and will support him during his recovery.

Happy running everybody and Vin and Jim, you win!

September 20th - Experience and belief. both very useful allies!

Well I had three runs this week, two on the road and 1 on the dreadmill. On Sunday I decided to retrace my Oggie run for a steady 5K and suitably kitted out I hit the road. It was awful, my legs felt heavy, my breathing was poor and although I finished in the same time roughly as the week before I did not enjoy it at all.

BUT!!!! Experience is a wonderful thing and I know you have bad runs, so I was not unduly upset at all as I know there will be good runs to come. When I looked at my stats I had started off way to quickly and as it is an uphill start I did not settle at all later into the run. So, Tuesday was a dreadmill session and I decided to run steady at around 9min a mile pace and relax through the run. It was not a difficult run and 27 minutes passed reasonably quickly given the TVs on the wall and my iPod playing running music in my ear.

Belief, I knew I had made mistakes, but I remember from last year that I do have a tendency to go off too fast and need to ease into the run, I know because of the advice and support on here, I am a better runner because of it.

Back early from work, but a parent's evening to attend I was unable to pop to the gym, so I decided to try a road run again. It was warm so I put on my NASS vest, cars can see you a mile off, and set off steadily easing into a 10 minutes a mile pace. It was an easier run up the hill to the first turn and then I settled into my usual pace of around 9:30 minutes a mile for the middle stages before pushing onto 9 minutes a mile at the end. It was good, my legs are still not road conditioned yet, very heavy still, but I know that will improve, but my breathing was fine and the knee was good and I felt comfortable knowing that when I'm ready I should be able to ease the mileage up.

Like Vin it is three steps forward and two steps back, I still feel tightness in my right thigh muscle from the sciatica which slows me a bit, but I am hoping that with regular stretching and looking after my back it will eventually go? It means I am about 30 seconds a mile off my marathon pace, the one I feel comfortable with when on the road, but I am not unduly worried, things are moving in the right direction and I'm not going to rush it. I am concerned that the sciatica is still there, although not anywhere near as bad as it was back in February, but has anybody tried Acupuncture for their various injuries as it is something I have been told might help, but I'm a bit sceptical?
Anyway, lovely weather for running and I enjoyed today knowing that pretty soon the winter training will be upon us. I remember how cold it was last year as I pounded the roads so today was a bonus.
Lastly it is almost time for the ballot results for VLM 2014 which will be out soon so fingers crossed for everybody and happy running.

September 24th - Broke down today.......

Well Real Buzzers, I felt good even though the knee was a bit sore for some reason, not anywhere near the site of the operation, but I decided to venture out onto the road instead of the gym as it was a balmy evening and there will not be many of those left.

As it was dark I wore my NASS vest and headed off into the night on my usual 5K run. I set off slowly, but after a mile I was beginning to push a bit and the legs were feeling good, breathing was fine and only the odd twinges from the knee, hip and back which in true Hollywood style I pushed to the back of my mind.

I began to really enjoy the run, something I have not done for a long time and was able to run freely clocking the sights and sounds around instead of concentrating on putting one foot on front of the other. This was good, this is what I run for, and then I broke down.

I didn't stop running; I didn't need to as I broke down in tears! I broke down as it hit me why I had begun this, why I had started to train for the marathon, why I had pushed myself to an injury. I run because I am running for Neil, I am running for my brother, I am running for the brother I lost to cancer 18 months ago, I am running because he couldn't and every step I run I run for him

So I ran through the tears feeling a bit of an idiot, but no one noticed the guy in the orange vest with tears trickling down his face, why should they. I ran on and I ran well and I felt stronger because of it, the time wasn't anything special, but the feeling was good, I wasn't out of breath and I wasn't aching. I am obviously ready to move up through the miles, but I will be patient and wait until my 5K is even more comfortable, a warm up if you will and then I will push on a mile at a time towards that goal, towards London in April and running for Neil.

I never forget the title of my blog and why I started it, why I am doing it, but as my injuries begin to fade in the memory and I am getting stronger I find myself thinking as I run and the grief just hit me tonight. I know it will from time to time and I'm not ashamed to admit I miss him terribly, but he is not forgotten and I will be there on that start line come hell or high water and I will wear his name with pride on my vest.

Good luck in the ballot everyone who has entered and happy running.

From: Neil Adam
To: John Adam
Sent: Mon, 28 March, 2011 23:18:24
Subject: Palsy

Hi John,

The steroids have stopped my Palsy lip droop but I still have some deafness in my left ear. They are going to do an MRI head scan as a precaution so this might be later this week or next .Of course it's a worry but I feel pretty good this week and the Steroids have also increased my appetite so I don't mind my legs being a bit swollen! The house build is getting quite exciting now as we finalise the kitchen design and start to talk about the boundaries and landscaping.

One of the things that kept my brother going during his illness was a project to build a house on the land they owned at the back of their existing home. It was planned to be something for his retirement, but circumstances now dictated that it was a race to complete in time so that Neil would be able to spend some time living in it. Over the last year I had viewed many plans and listened to him explain the various details, but now it was nearing completion and was a great focus for him.

The original design of the house had to be altered to accommodate the various issues Neil had with mobility and so that was something to keep him busy organising. There was a wet room downstairs with wheelchair access and an electronic ramp to move him from the kitchen to the lounge where his bed was installed. From there would be a glorious view over the valley where they lived. I am convinced that Neil lived longer than expected because of his determination to see his project through.

16 LIFE GETS IN THE WAY AT TIMES.

October 6th - Apologies Real Buzzers and thanks Jim!

Since my last post it's been an interesting couple of weeks and I have neglected the Real Buzz community unfortunately. Thanks to Jim for asking how I was and giving me the push I needed. Like everybody else I was keen to see if I had got in through the ballot, but unfortunately I was not successful, but I have my place with Cancer Research UK so it is back to fund-raising.

In short I began to feel a few twinges around my knee last week and so, after reading Vin's blog I decided to rest it and not run this week. Then my younger son got into a bit of trouble at school and everything has been on hold since then. I have read a few blogs, but my mind has been elsewhere and I was worried about my knee.

We are sorting out the school business, suffice to say it will be a life lesson for a teenage boy and one that has been coming, although it has caused no end of stress, such is life!

So I ventured out for golf today and there were no problems (with the knee, not my golf I hasten to add!!) and after a quick drink I decided to go for a road run. As I got changed I checked my Garmin and glanced on my PC screen to see a message from Jim asking if I was okay. What timing and how thoughtful as it gave me the boost I needed to get back out there, many thanks Jim, appreciated.
The run was good, I settled into a steady pace at the beginning and eased though one mile and then two quite comfortably and pushed the pace up a bit for the third mile, mindful of the need to consider how I will feel when I start to push the mileage up.

I seem to be a steady 9:20 miler, although I have consciously slowed down to just under 10:00 to make sure I am comfortable, but my pace seems to increase until I'm running at 9:30 so I make a point of checking my Garmin regularly.

I know I could run faster and further, but like Vin, I'm not going to as I need to be realistic. Could I run a four hour marathon, possibly, but I think I may have to adjust my targets to match my various issues I have with a recently operated on knee and a stubborn case of sciatica.
Neither of these affects my running style, but I am aware of them and I think they stop me from running freely. My knee will improve, I am doing

stretches and strengthening exercises to keep everything stable and I hope that the sciatica will eventually go. I have six months, fingers crossed.

So I'm feeling more positive today and will read through a few more blogs as well, always good to see how others are doing and, as this time last year, it's back to training seriously now with that April goal in mind.
Good running everybody.

October 16th - Can't let life get in the way!!

As some of you have gathered, bit of a crisis regarding my youngest son these last two weeks which has caused a bit of a setback in my running. I have been driving into work instead of cycling, not been out on the roads as much as I wanted to and struggled to get to the gym.

I got back from work yesterday and there was another problem with my oldest son, nobody told me raising teenagers was so difficult, I have two 'Kevins' living in my house and nothing I do or say makes any difference to the way they behave, it's exasperating and wearing to say the least!

Anyway, I decided last night to get to the gym and have some time for me; wife was okay with that so off I went. Stretched carefully and then decided on a steady 3 miles on the treadmill at around 9:00 a mile pace. I did the first mile in 9:00 with no problems, knee was fine and I'd stretched the sciatica out so I pushed the pace up a bit and completed the second mile in 8:15 and still felt comfortable so I pushed the pace up again for the last mile and did that in 7:45 finishing in 25 minutes which is the second time I have run 3 miles in 25 minutes since the op.

Knee was fine, the odd twinge, but I've since learnt to push past those HD style and the sciatica was not too bad, breathing was fine and although it was only 3 miles I'm starting think about pushing on further and what pace to run at. At the moment I'm trying to get some conditioning back in the legs and lungs without getting injured again, but around December I shall start increasing the distances, slowly this time though.

So all in all feeling pleased, but still unable to run in any local runs although I am sure I will be able to after the Christmas break. Enjoying the blogs, family problems have meant less time for running and blogging though as the title says, I'm not going to let life get in the way as the Real Buzz community has become quite an important part of running nowadays.

Good running everybody!

October 2oth - Planning for the big day in April!

Hi all, only made time for a couple of runs this week, one at the gym and one on the road and whilst out running yesterday I had a big smile on my face as I began to formulate a plan for my training. The run on the road was a nice easy jog as I had planned to try marathon pace and see how I felt. At the gym I push harder, but on the road, conscious that I will need to push on at some stage, I take it much easier.

So took it steady for the first mile, but still came in under 10 minutes and felt fine and started to enjoy the run and look around a bit more to take in the various sights and sounds of the day. It was then that I realised that there will be plenty of people lining the roads in April and what that might feel like? I began to feel motivated like never before and tried to visualise running along the streets of London with crowds cheering you on.

That's my goal of course, to run for my brother, for Cancer Research UK, but also for me, it's something I have dreamed of doing for a long time. So then I began to work out my training plans, aware of the fact I will need to put the mileage in soon, but stay injury free this time!

Eventually I worked out the following and by this time I was well into my third mile and feeling okay. I seem to settle into a steady 9:30 per mile pace as I've said before and that is fine, I'd like to be 30 seconds a mile quicker, but it's a comfortable pace for me and one I feel I can maintain as the miles increase. So, I am going to run three times a week, twice at the gym doing core strengthening work and 3 miles on the treadmill at various speeds and then one road run that increases by 10% every week, slowly building up to 20 miles.

I realise that is only one long road run a week, but I pushed too hard too fast last year and look where it got me? I will also be cycling a few times a week, walking a great deal and playing golf when I can. I think that will work for me, I certainly hope so, but if anybody sees a flaw in my plans then feel free to let me know, I'm grateful for any advice on here as I know it comes from people who know what they are talking about. Happy running everybody!

October 26th - Ten percent added this week.......

It's been half term this week and I have been at home doing various jobs around the house, but I was determined to get out as much as I could. It has been really warm as well which is a pleasant change from last year, so I have been able to get a couple of runs on the road as well as a couple of runs at the gym.

I have been trying to stretch out my knee which is still quite tight, I'm not able to bend it fully yet and sit with my legs tucked under me so I have also been doing a lot of stretching. Although I don't have the pain I used to get from within the knee, I do get some niggling aches which is quite irritating, but doesn't seem to affect my running?

Reading Jim's blog and referring to the Real Buzz baton for motivation made me smile, I also remind myself of the exploits of fellow Real Buzzers to push any negative thoughts away, especially if I am worried about my knee or my sciatica is playing up.

So today, the rain was chucking it down and it was blowing a bit, but with thoughts of Oggie and Rob running the Snowdonia marathon I got my gear on and set off. I wanted to run at marathon pace with thoughts of adding miles over the coming months, so I set off at a steady pace and settled into a comfortable rhythm. I was listening to Seasick Steve of all things as my iPod was out of charge so I was using my phone instead, but it was great music to listen to and I was feeling good.

Around 2 miles I started to think about moving the miles up and although I am not in any hurry I felt an extra ten percent would be fine and so planned to run a bit further. At that stage the lyrics of one of Seasick Steve's songs sounded quite poignant given where I am with my running and why I am doing it and as I approached 3 miles I felt good. I ran 3.3 miles exactly and then eased off for a cool down walk, checking my Garmin I was amazed to see I was still well under 9:30 a mile despite thinking I was running a bit slower so that was good and I really feel ready to move the miles up.

Oh, and those words that inspired me..........

"The least they can say when you're dead and gone, you never gave up you kept going on"

Sent: 31/05/2011 22:04
To: John Adam
Subject: Visit today

Hi John,

Have been told today that I need to go into a hospice for 2 weeks to spend 90% of my day off my bottom...bit of a bummer but if I don't the risk of infection now is quite high, they are breaking up into more holes. It could kill me before the cancer does so to speak so have really got no choice but to go with it. It will be hard but hopefully it will work. They will also carry on with the suction pump and have not ruled out a stand aid, but the priority is to get the pressure off quickly now.

Around this time Neil had to go into a hospice and this was a tremendous worry as he was seriously ill with complications from his bed sores, yet another indignity he had to endure. When we visited him I noticed quite a change in his demeanour, he looked a beaten man and I was concerned that he would spend his last days there. Yet remarkably he rallied again, the treatment was successful and he was soon in better spirits.

The visit itself was quite difficult as poor Neil had to be on his side and so his vision was restricted, but it was a lovely place and the nurse who looked after him was a lovely character, extremely cheerful and just the sort of person Neil needed to believe again. There seemed to be an increase in the number of problems he had to endure on a weekly basis, but he faced them all and came up smiling when a lesser individual would have succumbed much earlier.

17 THE DREADED CRAMP

November 10th - 3 steps forward - 2 steps back.....

Not been able to get on RB for quite a while, after two weeks half term it was back to school with a vengeance and the hectic countdown to Christmas. Observations, reports, new initiatives, it has been exceptionally busy at work and I've not had five minutes to post, but I have been reading all your blogs, albeit without commenting I'm afraid.

As well as a heavy workload my running has taken a bit of a back seat, due in part to working in the evening and also due to a minor injury unfortunately. In the first week of half term I went to the gym and after a longish warm up I set off on my usual 5k/3 miles on the treadmill. Felt quite good so I upped the pace and came in under 24 minutes for the run which is easily my best time for about 5 years! So feeling good I managed a road run later in the week of 3 miles and felt able to push on to 4 miles.

At 2 and a half miles my left calf suddenly popped, for no reason, but when I thought about it as I limped home I was not hydrated at all and therefore suffered the inevitable consequence. I was so annoyed with myself as everything was going so well and now my calf was really sore to the point that walking was quite difficult for a few days.

I iced, as well as massaged and walked everywhere for a week and the calf felt fine, so, a week later I stretched, drank and then set off. No real problems at all, pace was slow but steady and everything seemed okay until just before two miles the calf started to tighten again. I stopped and walked back and immediately iced the leg before having a hot bath and massaging the soreness out.

By now I was very annoyed and have been hoping that this would not be a long term injury; I have no time for cramp in my schedule so it needs to be managed properly. So back at work I have walked to work a few times and cycled the rest as well as making sure I have stretched and massaged the calf every day, but no running for a week. As of today, after a conference in London yesterday after which I walked from Paddington to Covent Garden and then back up to Oxford Circus before making my way down Regent Street to Waterloo, I am reasonably happy with the injury and feel I can try a run this week again, but I think a steady jog on the treadmill first.

I'm not happy with my running at the moment, yet when I am out walking the dog I'm itching to pick up the pace a bit and that is a good thing, I am still feeling positive about the marathon in April, I'm just not happy with my training at the moment, but I am being sensible. I am also cross with myself for getting cramp in the first place as it was completely avoidable if I had just followed a few basic rules. I had woken up with a headache which is unusual for me, but failed to recognise it as a sign of dehydration. Had a cup of tea which would have made the situation worse and then with minimal stretching and no compression socks I set off; I know better than that so I am annoyed I failed to follow any of the basic principles I have learnt over the last year.

Anyway, tomorrow's another day, very busy at work still and a parents' evening to attend (I'm presenting to the parents) reports to organise on Tuesday, another conference on Wednesday and youngest son needs taking to football training from 7:30 to 9:30 on Thursday; so no chance of any run until Friday but I shall be walking, cycling and stretching all week. Here's hoping this is just a minor setback and I can start to push the mileage up as I feel more than ready, both physically and mentally. Happy running everybody, weather is getting colder, stay warm!

November 15th - Not just once, but twice!

Today I ran four miles on the road, longest I have run on the roads since my injury back in January and feel I'm on my way back. I have been stretching every day since getting cramp and massaging the muscle as well as eating copious amounts of bananas. On Tuesday the calf felt good so I went to the gym, but wore my compression socks and running gear on the treadmill. Walking for the first 5 minutes I then upped the pace and ran a steady 4 miles in 39 minutes with no problems. No twinges, not cramping, just a steady run, I loved it, but it put doubts in my mind. Why was I cramping on the road, I have never cramped at the gym?

Anyway, today I left work early and was home by 12:30, stretched, massaged and ate a banana as well as drank some water and then donned my cold weather running gear, lycra leggings, CRUK T-Shirt and London marathon windcheater, compression socks, running beanie, running gloves (yellow) and Garmin! Warning middle-aged men in lycra, I must look a sight, but it is cold out there.

Anyway, I set off and all seemed well covering the first mile in 9:13 seconds which was a bit too fast given my issues with my calf so I eased back a bit and the next mile took 9:40 seconds which was better and no sign of any calf problems. My legs felt a bit heavy, but I put that down to the fact I had cycled to and from work which was hard work in windy conditions. So the third mile seemed fine as I realised that nothing was hurting save for the heavy feeling in my legs, my knee was fine, sciatica was not a problem, the calf was good and breathing was regular and not laboured at all. Third mile was covered in 9:37 seconds and then the last mile in 9:25 for an overall 9:29 per mile which I was very pleased with.

I felt quite happy at that pace and made sure I stretched when I got back and massaged the calf, but there has been nothing to indicate a problem yet, so I'm feeling quite pleased with myself. I now need to keep this 10% increase per week as steady as I can and listen to my body. Stretch, massage and make sure I am hydrated. Fittingly, the last song on my iPod as I was coming to the end of my run was Seasick Steve and the words I shall carry with me on all my runs, "the least you can say when I'm dead and gone, he never gave up he kept going on"

Today was a good day, happy running everybody!

November 20th - As the man said "done, not quick, but done"

There is a bug going round at work, if you work with kids like I do then it's a fact of life and today I felt really quite odd as if in a fog? So I took it as easy as I could, ended up covering 2 lessons for a colleague who was away sick, the irony!

Anyway, I digress, I read a few blogs whilst the time passed slowly and young Jim's struck me as rather apt, goodness know how he gets up at that godforsaken hour and runs, I have nothing but admiration for his determination. Thinking about it though, I was due a run at the gym on the way home, the usual 3 miler with some stretches and speed work, but had already decided to go home and lie quietly in a darkened room. Then I started to think about Jim's blog, he got it done, not fast, but he got it done, so I went and ran and took it steady at marathon pace. Did 3 miles in 27 minutes, not fast, but enough to keep me ticking over and enough to try and blow whatever I have got out of system. It didn't, but I don't feel any worse and I got a 3 miler under my belt, so thanks Jim.

That's the thing about this site though, it's like having a personal trainer sitting on your shoulder, I had every reason to go home and take it easy, just miss one run, why not, but you join Real Buzz and you become part of a running community, advice and support are always available as well as inspiration in spades.

I may not comment as much as I could, but I read as many blogs as I can, it's part of my daily routine. There is a reason behind every one on here and they make compelling reading. As if to confirm I had done the right thing, I got home to find my Cancer Research UK pack with my vest on the doormat! Good running everybody.

November 24th - Seasick Steve gets me to 5 miles!

Running has been good this week, never in my darkest days did I think I would be saying that, but it really has, the cold is a bit of a challenge, but like Vin last year I am pounding the dreaded treadmill and venturing out on the road only once a week and it seems to be working. As many of you know, I am a fan of Seasick Steve and use his music on my runs.

On Friday I set off on what I consider to be my marathon pace and then slowed down a bit with the idea of doing 4 miles, but felt fine after I reached 4 and so carried on to 5 miles with relative ease. Felt good about that and also that it was not a gasping for breath at the end but a feeling of more to come.

Legs were fine, no cramps, no knee pain, sciatica under control and I spent 30 minutes stretching afterwards then into the Steam Room, lovely! Anyway, woke up this morning and first thing I did was log onto RB and read Oggie's report.....wow, what a blog and what a man, incredible and hope he gets good news from the doctor.

Inspired by Oggie I decided to go out for a 3 miler and got kitted out, compression socks are a given nowadays as is the beanie and lycra leggings topped off with yellow running gloves, Garmin and headphones! I stretched for around 20 minutes, drank quite a bit of water and ate a banana and then off I went. Now I tried to settle into a slower pace than normal to see what my natural pace was, so I did not look at my Garmin and just enjoyed the run.

And I did, I enjoyed the run, no knee issues, no problems with the sciatica, no issues with any cramping, just me, Seasick Steve and the roads in reasonable harmony. I have started to think of the places I shall see on the way, but the Mall keeps popping into my head and the song they always play and I know I am on my way, 5 months to go, but I'm on my way.

I ran 3 miles easily and glanced down to see 9.30 pace per mile, a lot faster than I intended but it seems to be my natural plodding pace as I felt comfortable and so pushed on and ran another mile finishing in 38 minutes and knowing, as on Friday that I wasn't gasping for breath but feeling as if I could carry on. I won't though, it is 10% all the way and ease on through the miles, but I had a good run, I feel great and feel that things are starting to come together.

So thoughts turned to fund raising as my running vest and VLM pack arrived last week, so I posted on my Facebook page an update about why I am running for my brother Neil and a link to my just giving page and then logged on here to notice a message I missed from Jim about his cookbook. Great idea and the timing couldn't have been better, so thanks Jim and another reason why this site is just the best. I was trying to explain to somebody the other day about Real Buzz and how it was helping me in my running, but I couldn't find the words and I think you have to be part of it to understand it, I really do.

Anyway, today was a good day, may there be many more on the journey to April 13th, good running everybody!

From: Neil Adam
To: John Adam
Subject: Moving Target
Date: Mon, Jul 18, 2011 9:09 am

Hi John,

I am holding up well and although it's a struggle with all the drugs and treatments I hope to keep going like this until after the move and maybe into Christmas? Nobody can tell me really but so far my face is no worse and I have got used to feeling having just returned from the dentist! But I can still eat and enjoy it, so quite a relief.

Neil was beginning to believe he would be able to move into the new build and spend some quality time there. He continued to have various issues that needed adjustment to his drug regime, but he was coping well and managing to remain as positive as before. He had started to set himself small goals and was hoping he would see another Christmas. At this stage I still had not thought about the time he would no longer be around. With our mother, who was eighty when she passed away, it was a case of having lived a good long life and this was her time. We had time to prepare for her passing, but in Neil's case this was not something we had planned for.

All my thoughts were with my brother and how he was coping with the various health problems he had and I gave no thought to how I might deal with his passing. To a certain extent I was in denial and, as Neil did, expected him to carry on for some time yet.

18 IT'S THE SEASON FOR COLDS.

December 2nd - Hollywood style gets me to six miles on the road!

Well I missed my run on Thursday at the gym as I got a terrible streaming cold courtesy of the kids I work with (the downside of being a teacher, you pick up all sorts of bugs) so I sat in the steam room for half an hour. Cleared my head but sneezed my way through the next few days and felt awful by Sunday. I was due a 10% extra run, so looking at around 4 ½ miles on the road, but I felt too bad to get out and stayed in bed. The guilt, it's unbelievable but I needed to let my body recover.

Anyway, even though I felt under the weather I had an idea that stemmed from Hollywood's run when he was not so well. The cold was now on my chest and my legs felt really heavy, but I wondered how far I could run when feeling run down, it would be a good test of my body when things are tough. So, when I got back from work I put my running gear on, plus beanie, gloves etc., stretched for 20 minutes, ate a banana, drank some water and set off at a steady pace. It was cold, but my breathing wasn't laboured and I jogged slowly around the houses looking at all the Christmas lights and listening this time to Michael Buble!

At 2 miles I found a good rhythm and thought I could manage 3 miles, but at 3 I felt I would go for 4 and before long I had run for an hour and got to 6 miles, the furthest I have run since my injury back in January. It wasn't too tough, the legs were burning a bit, but any discomfort was dismissed as the joy at ticking off the miles. I was really pleased, as Jim would say, they were honest miles, not quick, but I felt I dug deep to push on and even though I stopped at six miles I had more in the tank, but I was aware that I was not fuelled for any further and I had a heavy cold.

So I feel in a good place right now, this time last year I was running for an hour and then pushed on up to 10 miles too quickly and suffered for it. It's 10% all the way, keep it steady and build strength in the legs. 3 miles is a warm up, 6 miles a short run and so on.

Back to the gym on Thursday and get a speed run in, but I am more of the opinion that I will plod round in April rather than force the pace, the sciatica does affect me unfortunately, it doesn't stop me running, but it does slow me down. Maybe it will have gone by then, who knows, but it has been like this now for nearly 10 months so I can't see much changing. Stretching helps, but it is always there and maybe I just have to learn to live with it.

On the plus side, the knee is fine; surgery has been a success thank goodness. Happy running everybody, keep warm.

December 9th - Getting stronger every run.

Well I really enjoyed reading about the exploits of the Real Buzz Park run this Saturday, it seemed like a fantastic team effort and as many have said I was gutted to have missed it. For sure there must be an event for all of us Real Buzzers to get together at some stage in the future, such camaraderie and many PBs, sounds like it was a brilliant day for everybody.

So, motivated after reading the blogs I decided to get a run in after all having spent the day travelling up to and back from Balham for family reasons and not really feeling like a run what with spending nearly 5 hours in the car most of which was getting through Tooting Bec! The inspirational stories of the Park Run proved a great motivator and I got my kit on after we got back and set off into the night for just a 3 mile jog. It was lovely to be out with all the Christmas lights on the houses, there seems to be more this year than ever and it was nice to run along the streets checking out the wonderful displays.

I started off quite steady and then began to wind it up a bit as I felt much stronger, stronger than I have on the road for a while anyway and before long I had gone through 3 miles with the last mile at 8:30 pace which is way too fast for longer runs, but I felt comfortable. I slowed down and cooled down very pleased to have got a run in as I intended to put it off to Monday. Woke up today feeling okay, not stiff and the knee was good although the sciatica always requires some stretching in the morning. It was a good day at work, busy as there are loads of end of term things to sort out, but I decided to get to the gym for another run as I felt good.

Now I have not run on two consecutive days for nearly a year, so this was quite a decision, but I felt it was something I could manage so I set off for another 3 mile run, but this time on the treadmill. It felt good again, an easy pace and 3 miles done in 28 minutes with no problems, knee good, sciatica not an issue, no sign of any cramp and comfortable with my breathing. I must admit I did stretch for around 20 minutes focussing on my piriformis, a muscle I have come to understand a lot over the last 10 months!

Finished with 20 minutes in the steam room, bliss and feeling very positive at the moment, even more so knowing I only have two days of work left. I know it is early days yet and there is still a way to go, but I feel more in control this time and I am taking it very steady, especially with the increase in distance. This week I hope to push my road run to 7 miles which is easily within my capabilities and then I hope to move through the miles from January onwards as evenly as possible. Unlike last year I won't be making huge advances, but I will increase the 3 mile interval runs. There are a couple of 10k runs I might enter and certainly I will be looking at a half marathon around February to March time, we shall see how the training is going. I used to be a sub 24 min 5k runner, but since my injury woes I have had to lower my goals and have realised that I am least 4 minutes slower than that now and that is okay. It's not been easy to accept, but it is what it is and I am comfortable running at that pace. Maybe I will dip under 25 minutes again, maybe not but the main thing is to get back out there and enjoy my running again, and I am. Good running everybody!

December 20th - Oggie gets me to 7 miles..........and then 8!!!

It's been a great week for running and the Real Buzz team have been producing some great runs, not least of which the amazing Oggie with back to back marathons and another one scheduled! I had a poor run last Friday, 4 miles and it was very windy, my legs were heavy and I felt out of sorts so I was a bit dispirited over the weekend though I knew what had been the problem, too rushed, too fast a pace and not enough preparation, but I finished in a reasonable time.

On Sunday I read Oggie's blog and it inspired me to get out there, but this time I made sure I was fully prepared. I had porridge early on in the day, kept my fluid intake up and stretched for 20 minutes, then set off for what I had hoped was an extra 10% run to take me to 7 miles. I started off very steadily and took it easy as I followed a route that I had taken a year ago. I was a little concerned as the last time I ran this route I cramped, badly, and that was the beginning of the end for me so I was trying to stay relaxed and focussed. I reached 3 miles with no problems and pushed on to 4, then 5 and then 6 so now I was in unknown territory and could feel some twinges here and there. I invoked the spirit of Hollywood and told all niggle to go away and pushed on to finish 7 miles in just under 70 minutes, not quick, but relaxed enough to know I was not exhausted.

The next day I thought I would try an easy session at the gym and covered 3 miles in just under 30 minutes at a really comfortable pace and then had a relax in the steam room. It was my intention to run again this week, but then my left foot started to ache and was tender by the arch which concerned me a bit. By today it had improved, but was still a bit sore and I think it is my trainers so I'm off to the sports shop after Christmas to get a decent pair for the New Year.

So, I thought I would try a 3 mile run at the gym today as the treadmill is easier on the feet and after a good stretch I set off at my intended marathon pace. It was comfortable running at that pace and inspired by young Vin I started to imagine where I might be at certain times, something I may look at for motivation and then 'The Trap' came on and that carried me onto to 4 miles without me even noticing. I then started to think about a 10k, 6 miles and got there easily enough before deciding to add the extra 10% and push through to 8 miles, almost a third of the distance to run in April. Got there in 75 minutes which I was really pleased with and I felt comfortable knowing that I could carry on, BUT I am sticking with my 10% rule or thereabouts. What was more pleasing was the fact that after a min my pulse was down to 80 BPM which is a good indication of how much fitter I am getting.

I am really pleased with that run, it's a bit faster than on the road, I always seem to be slower on the road for some reason, but it is all looking much more positive as we head towards the New Year. I have also found a really good piriformis stretch which seems to work for my sciatica and hopefully I can keep it at bay, maybe even get rid of it? My next target though is to get some decent trainers, I have done over 300 miles in this pair and although they are in good condition I think it is time to get measure up for a pair properly. The Real Buzz blogs have been truly inspirational this last couple of weeks and have really helped me, Hollywood Dave may not be around and getting some well-earned family time, but his support is still there and drives us all on. Have a great Christmas everybody, good running.

December 28th - Somehow I'm getting fitter and stronger, a PB for 3 miles!

I know this should be the case as I'm training 3 to 4 times a week and getting the mileage in, it's just hard to believe after last year's disappointment. I have managed a couple of runs this last week, but I have also eaten a little too much as well as drunk a fair bit, though I must admit most of it has been reasonably healthy. I just can't eat the quantities I used to and I don't seem to want to drink too much either. So although I have over-indulged it's not been too bad and the desire to get out and run has been ever present, which is a good sign.

On Boxing Day I went for a short 3 mile run just to keep things ticking over and ran at an average of around 9:30 which was comfortable. What was good though, I thought I'd add an extra mile to keep the mileage up for the week and did 4 miles with relative ease? The ability to keep plodding along at a reasonable pace is something I have been working on and it seems that I am able to keep the pace up and knock off the miles, albeit only to 8 miles so far. I don't feel exhausted at the end; I just stop and cool down, mindful of my 10% rule. I do have a plan now and one which I feel should work for me given the issues with my knee and sciatica, but things are gearing up for a great run on the big day in April and I am feeling positive.

So after another family do yesterday, 11 people round for lunch and buffet tea, I was determined to get a run in at the gym. Set off this morning with a speed session in mind so I set the runner at a good pace only to realise I had got my figures wrong and I was running at under 7 minutes a mile. I felt okay though so carried on and thought I would ease up later, but I got halfway still feeling quite strong, so I carried on. I got to 3 miles in 20:59 sec, the fastest I have ever run 3 miles and have no idea how I did it. I did not feel too exhausted though my legs knew they had worked hard so I am very pleased with that.

I was a sprinter back in the day, long distances have not come easy to me, but even so I am amazed that at the age of 56 I have run 3 miles faster than I ever could in my youth. I can only conclude that I am much fitter and stronger than this time last year, even though I was running further.

This is good news and means I can maintain my 10% increase week by week and know that I not only have endurance but also speed. Since the knee op I have taken things steady and have built a great platform for the serious training in the New Year. I am looking forward to the months ahead, but I'm also mindful that I am not alone, there are many of us here on Real Buzz who all have goals they have set themselves for 2014.

Here's to a great year and some great running, Happy New Year to all of you that have followed my story and supported me on what has become an incredible journey. Your stories have inspired me and moved me in equal measure.

From: Neil. Adam
To: John Adam
Sent: Monday, 1 August, 2011 20:47:49
Subject: It's working OK

Hi John,

Its 5 30 and not much pain I can feel yet, so much better than yesterday what a relief only gave me one top up and one IV paracetemol during the night so that looks to be the way forward on pain control now if stick to tablets they can do that at home They may not let me go home today, I will have to see what they say later. Bowels also not working yet again since Friday but then not eaten much because of the pain. Hope to see you soon at home, I am still fighting on after all these setbacks but am determined to see the house finished and us moved in OK so can enjoy the views in the rest of the summer, and I haven't ruled out Christmas yet.

Another hospital visit for Neil with some complications again, but very soon an email arrived letting me know that everything was okay and he was possibly going back home again soon. Despite everything he took these regular hospital visits in his stride and kept himself busy making plans for the new house.

Combatting the pain was a big challenge and I found that hard to bear as I hated to see his discomfort. I remember our mother howling in pain before the drugs kicked as she battled cancer. Yet he continued to deal with every health issue displaying a remarkable degree of stubbornness. This unwillingness to give in drove him on and Christmas in the new house seemed to be possible.

19 NOT THE BEST CONDITIONS.

January 5th - Running in the wind and rain!

The man-flu has lingered on this week and is now on my chest so I've restricted myself to a couple of gentle runs at the gym. This time last year I was keen to force the pace and ended up deferring my place, so I'm a little bit more sensible this time. Been reading the blogs on Real Buzz and they are truly inspirational, what with Hollywood's stirring post through to Oggie's amazing mileage it has been great to read how everybody is getting out there and running in pretty awful conditions.

My own running has suffered a setback with this cold (man-flu sounds worse) but I have been careful and run when I felt able to. I was due a 9 miler today and felt capable until I saw the weather! We have already lost a few roof tiles, one of which smashed my wing mirror, and have quite a few leaks due to storm damage. I was hoping it might ease off, but it has rained all day and continues to gust quite strongly at times. With quite a chesty cough I thought about running tomorrow, but it is the first day back at work and I have a presentation to give to the staff as well, it will be a busy day.

The day passed slowly and I read a few more blogs, Bexdragon feeling the pressure as the days count down, JennyMcc and her PB with Rob, Ruddy and his Turbo Trainer, Jim and his half-marathon, Red Dave who seems to have entered every race in 2014 and finally Rob and the Park Run with Jenny. All very entertaining as well as inspiring and of course you get that urge to get out there, that niggle at the back of your mind that you can't ignore.

So it was at 5:00pm I started getting 'the gear' on, CRUK vest, compression socks, lycra leggings, yellow reflective top, extra pair of running socks, trainers, beanie, yellow gloves, iPod and Garmin! I don't feel stupid anymore, I feel prepared nowadays as I know I need everything I have on. Stretched carefully for 20 minutes whilst my Garmin found a satellite and then set the iPod up. I know Hollywood has regaled us with his eclectic choice of music, mine is a combination of songs I know will motivate me and others that are great to run to.

I figured that I would just run 3 miles as it was blowing quite a gale and the rain was chucking it down, but I was determined to get a run in so off I set. Started off easily with 'Caliban's Theme' from Isles of Wonder, the tune they played at the Olympics, it means I don't start too quickly and is quite inspirational. The first part of the run is uphill, so I take it steady, but with the wind and rain I was having to force the pace a bit just to stay moving. Anyway, as I rounded the corner Pharell Williams came on and 'Happy' which is a great song, but also brilliant for pace keeping as it perfectly matches my stride. I carried on for another two miles and settled into what I call my marathon pace, only I had eased back a bit as the wind was quite strong in places.

I reached three miles easily enough so carried on as Tears for Fears played 'Everybody Wants to Run the World' which is also another great one to run to. I was quite happy at my pace, my legs felt okay, not out of breath, but I was conscious that I was still quite chesty and so decided to go for 4.5 miles which was half of what I should have done. Given the fact that I was not 100% and it was blowing quite a gale and I was soaked I think that was acceptable, I'm not so hard on myself anymore and next week I can aim to get the 9 miles completed, maybe even more, I feel capable. 'The Trap' started to play and it is amazing what effect that has as I moved through 4 miles and onto finish in around 45 minutes. Not quick at all, but as Jim would say, honest miles and given the conditions I'm not disappointed.

So, back to work tomorrow and hopefully this cold will clear completely and I can focus on pushing the mileage up. It's been a great holiday, despite the various coughs and colds, and there is an amazing Real Buzz spirit about at the moment, 2014 will be an incredible year I am sure.

January 10th - Double figures at last!

Inspired by the blogs of various Real Buzzers and mindful of the need for a longer run on the road I planned to get out today although I had a dentist appointment at 3pm. Fortunately I was able to get off work early and get home around 12:00 where I had laid my kit out ready (I find that tends to focus the mind) I am a bit behind my schedule due to this wretched man-flu which meant I had missed my 9 mile run last week and also I have had a few niggles from my sciatica which is a bit disappointing.

Anyway, no excuses, as Jennymcc, Vin, Bex, Jim, Gaelle and quite a few others had noted, it is sometimes hard and you have to dig in. That's where our own Hollywood comes in with words of encouragement, the inspirational running of Oggie and the incredible challenges many of you have set yourself in 2014.

As you all know, my chief aim, my only goal, is to run the London Marathon for Cancer Research UK in memory of my brother Neil and although I had to defer my place last year due to a series of debilitating injuries I am back on track and looking forward to lining up with many of the Real Buzz fraternity on April 13th.

So I kitted myself out and stretched, the weather was behaving itself so I planned a series of 3 laps of 3 miles although I took some jelly babies with me. Setting off steadily I got to the first turn off point and decided to go for a longer lap and carried on. The sciatica does not stop me running, but it does not help and I try to block it out though I have dropped my pace a bit to accommodate the tightness in the right thigh.

Anyway, I got to 5 miles easily enough, breathing was fine, knee was fine though I do find that my legs feel quite heavy, but I am convinced that is because of my trainers which are past their best now. There is no bounce in them at all and consequently I feel a bit flat-footed. I am off to a local specialist shop on Sunday for a bio-mechanical assessment and not a moment too soon as I don't think I can run on the road again in those trainers, it would be silly to do so!

So I pushed on regardless and then the wind started to blow and I found myself thinking of maybe shortening the run, for about 5 seconds, as I remembered the many blogs I had read about pushing on past our comfort zone, gritted my teeth and carried on. The rain started next, but that was not a major issue and even a bit refreshing as I headed onto the area where I cramped badly 12 months ago. Sailed past, plodded past I should say as it was a bit strong by now, and got to 8 miles okay. The thought of a possible 10 miles made me push on instead of heading back home and I got to double figures in 1 hour 40 minutes, not fast at all and my legs were feeling the effects by now, but that is the furthest I have run on the road for nearly a year.

I drank quite a bit of water when I got in and had a few bananas before showering and then cleaning my teeth for the dreaded dentist! By the time I sat in the dentist chair my legs were quite stiff, but when I got back I had a hot bath and then walked the dog which was a great way of stretching out tired legs. I am pleased to get to double figures, but not so happy with the time or how my legs feel, but I am sure that a decent pair of trainers will make quite a difference, I hope so anyway. Plodding along at that pace will give me a time of around 4 ½ hours which is slower than I would have wanted, but with the knee and the sciatica I have to be realistic.

I also got some good news regarding my fund-raising which I was beginning to worry about; we have a number of Jazz concerts at school to raise money for various causes as our head of music and her husband are professional Jazz musicians as well as teachers. They told me today that they would split the proceeds of the next concert 50/50 which will be a welcome boost for me. I am very grateful to them and I also intend to run a sweepstake on the night to guess my time. Hopefully I will be able to raise a reasonable amount, I hope so as last week I lost another family member to cancer and the more money I can raise for Cancer Research UK the better.

There has been some great blogs this week and I am sorry that I am unable to enter any of the many events some of you have signed up for, I have to be realistic and get to the start line in good health and able to get round, but after that, who knows?

January 19th - Trainers good, Flu bad!

Been reading the blogs with interest this week as everybody is getting some fantastic long runs in, which has inspired me and filled me with dread in equal measure. Am I doing enough, will my body cope with the extra mileage, what about my fundraising target….. It all adds to the feeling of inadequacy at times, but I know what my target is and I feel positive enough that I can get round, it's just that I want to get round in a good way, does that make sense?

Anyway, after last week's ten mile run I was feeling good, though there was a realisation that my trainers were shot and I really felt my quads the next day. That also made me cross as I have been slowly building up, mindful of the knee and sciatica and I knew I needed new trainers. I was hoping that I had not done any damage at all as I was still feeling the 10 miles on Sunday morning. I had already planned to get down to a specialist sports shop, but was concerned I may not be able to run properly in order to assess me therefore rendering the whole process a waste of time and money?

In the end I ventured down to Portsmouth and spent 3 hours in a shop filled with running wonders! I spent an hour perusing the shelves of running aids and wondered how we ever, as humans, ran before it became such an exact science? I read many running magazines as I awaited my turn, such is the enthusiasm for running that I was number 13 in the queue and watched as each person in turn was assessed, each one trying on many pairs and then running up the road and back again, quite comical really! Eventually it was my turn and apparently I have a good running style, balanced evenly, so I needed a pair that were neutral, but gave me a lot of cushioning to protect the issues I have with my knees. I ran up and down the road sometimes on my own, sometimes with other runners and eventually decided on a pair of Brookes Glycerin which were incredibly comfortable, but offered me a fantastic amount of cushioning from the road.

I was pleased with both the assessment and the choice of shoe which just happened to be on offer and I also purchased some running socks which were on a 2 for 1 offer, but still managed to get everything for just shy of £100.00 which was a bit of a bargain. I wore them round the house for the rest of the day and they felt brilliant and on Monday I went for a run at the gym to wear them in a bit, however I was just beginning to get a hint of this damn flu back again, the downside of working with kids, they are full or germs!

I planned a long run on Friday afternoon however and hoped that I would be okay, I had worked out a three mile course to do four times and then a bit further if I felt fine, but by Friday it was obvious I was not in a good enough shape. I set off anyway feeling reasonably positive, but after two miles I was struggling to breathe and decided to jog slowly round to finish after 3 miles and not push on as I didn't want to do any lasting damage. The right choice I felt and one positive to come out of such a short run was that the trainers were brilliant and well worth the money and time, but I was gutted that I couldn't get a longer run in.

I have read a few other blogs today and quite a few Real Buzzers have had some issues and I know I am not alone in my frustrations. It is what it is, I need to wait until this has cleared off my chest and then build up slowly again, knowing that I have done a reasonable amount of training and I have time. Last year at this time I was on my back in agony and my problems had just started, I'm in a different place this time around and feel positive. Happy running everybody!

January 26th - Back on track......sort of.....it all counts though!

It's been an interesting week to say the least and although I'm feeling much more positive about my training this has been tempered by the loss of another one of my family to cancer. My uncle had been having chemotherapy and was given the thumbs up before Christmas. We assumed all was well, but he went downhill rapidly just before the New Year and passed away two weeks ago. The funeral was on Tuesday, he was only 73 and full of life, a great character and I shall miss him a lot. Having lost so many friends and family to cancer he was passionate in his loathing for the disease and would always ask everybody to donate to Cancer Research rather than buy him a gift. For that reason, rather than purchase flowers his family had asked people to make a donation and I will be honoured to do so in his memory.

So although I am running for my brother Neil in April, I will be thinking of my uncle and indeed the many others who have succumbed to cancer. It will be a very emotional run and one I am determined to complete so I have been a little worried by my lack of training these last few weeks due to the dreaded man-flu.

It shifted to my chest at the beginning of the week and has been slowly improving, but I have been wary of getting back out there until I felt able to run freely. An opportunity arose on Thursday as I always take my son to football training and then either walk the dog for an hour or sit in the car and read. I thought I might get kitted out and then head off for an hour long run and duly did so. Now my son trains at a local school which is right out in the sticks and surrounded by fields and trees which meant I would be running mostly in the dark so I made sure I could be seen!

It was an interesting run as it turned out to be a hill trial and really made me work hard. As I set off up the hill my pace dropped and I really began to feel it in my legs, but pushed on to the brow of the hill and then turned left towards complete darkness. As I ran through the country lanes I came across a few houses with the odd light on, but everything was strangely quiet and at one stage I began to worry if I was headed in the right direction. Eventually I made it to the main road which took me back to the school and as I was feeling okay I then headed up the hill again! In all I managed 5 miles quite comfortably although the time was nothing special, but I was pleased I was back out there and also that the trainers were proving to be excellent purchase.

So this weekend I thought about a longer run on Sunday, maybe even 12 miles, but on Sunday morning it was absolutely pouring and quite windy. Normally I would have got out there, but mindful of the need to get rid of this cold I headed to the gym. An hour on the treadmill and 6 miles covered I was feeling relatively happy with the run. I had started slow covering 3 miles in 35 minutes and then pushed the pace up to cover the next 3 miles in 25 minutes which didn't leave me in any distress at all, but I was bored and looking out the window I noticed that it had at last stopped raining and the sun was actually out, so I got in my car drove the short distance home and headed out for another three miles on the road! I felt okay and settled into what I think will be my marathon pace now, I am still troubled by the sciatica which means I don't have as much power in my right leg and so have to compensate by slowing the pace a bit. I think I'm looking at a 4 hour 30 min marathon, but given my injuries this last year I would be happy with that.

I could have run on, but the clouds darkened again and it started to rain again, but I was happy with my form, happy with my trainers on the road and happy that I had actually pushed the mileage back up again, albeit in a split manner, but it all counts doesn't it? I feel okay at the moment, although I may be feeling the quads tomorrow, but in general I feel that I am back on track. It is definitely better for me to run at the gym and then attempt the long runs on the road and my next goal will be a half marathon and I feel that I can manage that comfortably enough in the next week or so.

From: Neil Adam
To: John Adam
Sent: Saturday, 24 September 2011, 18:16
Subject: New House

Dear John,

Do you want to come and see us in the new house next week or weekend? Forecast is good too. I have now recovered from a bout of infections, had a few grotty days but back fighting again. Am having some more pain at the moment, doctor says it's no indication of increased cancer activity but it hurts a lot when we use the hoist so it's annoying and I have to use Oramorph again to get through it, which makes me tired.

So at last the new house was finished and Neil and Linda moved in which was great news. This gave him a great boost in terms of his state of mind and increased his determination to stay around longer and enjoy the new surroundings. Pain was still an issue which meant he was more reliant on the drugs to get him through the day, but at least he was in the house, a project he had dreamed about for many years and one which he had seen through to completion.

I gave him time to settle in, although they were not moving far, there was still a lot of things to organise and of course as Neil was unable to do anything, it was down to Linda to organise which was quite some task. When I did eventually get up to see him it was good to see how relaxed he was. The house had an airy feel about it and although it was set up specifically for Neil it was a lovely place for him to relax and I just hoped that he had more time to enjoy it.

20 INCREASING THE MILEAGE

February 2nd - 13.1 miles at last, though not without some issues!

Well, reading Jennymcc and her inspirational blog got me into the right frame of mind for my LSR this Sunday. I am a little bit behind and needed to get a half marathon in this weekend, just to see where I stood. Some Real Buzzers have experienced a few niggles here and there and some are beginning to question whether they can make it round the course on April 13th, me included and so Jenny's blog was timely to say the least as she has run it and she knows what it feels like.

Nevertheless, inspired though I was I was still heading into unknown territory having never gone beyond 10 miles in training. I wore my Camelbak for the first time and carried some jelly babies and my phone in case I needed assistance at any stage! Anyway, it was a lovely day and I set off at a reasonable pace though after checking my Garmin later I realised it was a bit too fast. This was meant to be at a minute slower than my marathon pace, but I was running much quicker though I hardly noticed as the miles went by.

I had a slight crisis at 4 miles when I started to feel a bit rough and this was the beginning of my problems which were entirely self-inflicted. I was suffering from stomach cramps, though these passed after six miles, but I realised that it was not a good idea to have eaten two curries, a cheesecake and drunk two large glasses of wine the day before! You see I was at work and the chef had produced some excellent food which it would have been a crime to turn down and then my wife produced another excellent curry in the evening. I didn't really think about the next day's run as I had it in mind to get up at a reasonable time and have a bowl of porridge before letting my breakfast go down and setting off around two hours later, which I did though it was a bit later than I anticipated as my stomach was turning cartwheels.

I put that down to nerves, now I know better and at 9 miles I was desperate for the toilet which I had anticipated as my route took me past my house after 10 miles. That last mile was a long one, but I popped in, did what was necessary and set back off for the last three miles. They were not easy however and I struggled to get the pace back up again as my stomach was less than happy which in turn made me feel pretty low and lacking in any energy. I pushed on however and got to 13 miles eventually feeling pretty cross with myself for not thinking about nutrition and how important it is to fuel the body correctly.

Anyway, lesson learned and I will do better next time as I felt okay plodding along and could see no problem in moving the miles up until I got problems with my stomach. When I looked at my Garmin later it told a sorry story, my pacing was way off at the beginning and I then slowed at the 9 mile mark before finishing off the last three miles in a much slower time than I would have liked. All in all a Half Marathon in 2:15 with a rather uncomfortable period in the middle and a toilet stop, not good, but not bad either and another milestone achieved, though 20 years ago I ran the Portsmouth Half Marathon in 1:49 so I have lost over a minute each year! Have a good week everybody, enjoy your running!

February 9th - Fundraising boost AND 14 miles covered!

Friday was a fundraising night, as you know I work in a school where the Director of Music and her husband are also professional Jazz musicians and they have some amazing contacts. As well as a number of talented musicians appearing they also have quite a few performances from the children themselves. A clever move as their parents always attend; and as there is a bar and a plea for donations to different causes they always raise a lot of money.

They put on regular concerts throughout the year and I had asked if they would consider helping my fundraising efforts out. They had no hesitation in planning an event for this Friday with half the proceeds going to Cancer Research UK through my Just Giving account. The guest musician this time was Mark Armstrong, Professor of Jazz at the Royal College of Music and the school Hall was jam packed. He was particularly impressive and as a Jazz lover I really enjoyed his performance. I had expected to add another two hundred pounds or so to my total so far, but they had also planned to auction an old grand piano and announced that half the proceeds would also go to me. They called me up and I spoke about why I was running the London Marathon and how my training was going. As a teacher I am used to talking in front of people, but I was a little nervous as I was conscious of the fact that this was another stage in my journey to run the marathon in honour of my brother Neil.

Now I know nothing about pianos, but this was a grand piano that had been restrung and tuned and was in good condition, but I had no idea of what it might go for? Bidding started at 99 pence and an eager hand shot up; then it slowly moved to £100, then £200 and before I knew it had reached a £1000! I was over the moon as that meant my total was now nearer £1500 and much closer to the £2000 I needed. It didn't stop there and incredibly it was eventually sold for over £1900 and I was speechless. I was beginning to get a bit worried about my total so far and had begun to plan for various activities like cake sales and guess my time, but this takes the pressure off and lets me concentrate on my training, brilliant, and I am so grateful to everybody involved.

As for my running, well it's been a good week as I have looked to concentrate on 10 min mile pace and get used to running at that pace for longer. I have been running at the gym as the weather has not been good at all, but also I am conscious of the need to protect the various issues I have and not get injured so close to the day. A short run is now an hour and I am comfortable holding that pace, no niggles, although I do stretch for at least 20 minutes beforehand. I learnt a lot last week and so on Saturday, after the morning at work I headed to the gym to see how far I could run with only porridge for breakfast some 5 hours previously. I was fine until 4 miles and then started to feel my energy levels drop, so a good lesson for me in terms of nutrition. In the evening I had a really healthy meal of chicken and pasta, no alcohol and a banana and in the morning I had a big bowl of porridge.

Now I had read Jenny's blog with interest which had made me think about my LSR as she met up with various people along the way. I don't have that luxury, but given the weather I thought I might split the run into sections and do part on the treadmill and part on the road. It was blowing a real gale, so I did an hour at the gym and ticked off 6 miles at marathon pace before setting off on the road for 4 miles and then back to the gym for the last 4, boom, 14 miles in all although the 4 miles on the road were really hard as I was battling the wind all the way.

Still I feel really positive now, the pressure to raise £2000 for Cancer Research UK is now off and I can start to really enjoy my running and get my body ready for April 13th.

February 17th - Those must be comfortable shoes.......

My new trainers are excellent, really comfortable and have made running much easier, but I have other issues which may, or may not, have an answer. This is one for the men, though ladies feel free to offer an opinion! I am not sure quite what to wear under my running shorts and have had some rather uncomfortable runs lately due to some rubbing issues. I have tried wearing shorts with sewn in material to hold everything in place as it were, but they have proved to be a problem after an hour due to sweating. I have tried Speedos, but they have caused some soreness as well, so this week I tried some tighter undershorts which seemed to be okay, but I still had some problems later in the run, which leads me to ask the question, what do you guys wear underneath your shorts?

As I am going on much longer runs now I don't want to worry about rubbing in areas where I would rather there was none, if you get my meaning, so any advice is appreciated!

I had a golfing trip this weekend which has been planned for some time so I knew there would be no LSR on Sunday and made sure I racked up the miles last week with a number of tempo runs at the gym. The weather has been so foul that I have taken to getting on the treadmill for an hour at a time with no rest day in between to get used to setting a steady pace concentrating on staying relaxed. I know it is not as good as outside on the road, but I need to make sure I get to this start line in one piece and if the dreadmill is the way to do it then that is what I will do. I covered well over 30 miles last week which doesn't sound a lot, but as I'm covering 6 miles in an hour that is nearly a run a day to make that total, so I am pleased with my commitment if nothing else. I am also on half term now so I know I can get a couple of road runs in this week during the day, weather permitting.

Talking of weather, after all the gales and rain we have had I was not convinced that I would be playing any golf at all, but it would seem fortune favours the brave as the last two days have been sunny, warm and with only a light breeze. So lucky to get two rounds of golf in such beautiful conditions and as it was quite a hilly course I was pleased with my stamina over the 36 holes played.

Anyway, I ate as healthily as was possible and was careful with my alcohol intake, though the full English breakfast this morning was probably not that good for me, but I'm sure it will not do me any lasting damage! Rest day today and then back to some running tomorrow at the gym and then a LSR on Wednesday. I also have a deep tissue massage booked on Friday followed by some osteopathy. I find the sciatica does hinder me on my longer runs and am hoping that something can be done before April. They are also going to advise me on whether acupuncture might help, we shall see, but I am willing to try anything at this stage. I can't really afford too many sessions, but feel it is something I should explore.

So, good running everybody and if anybody has any advice as to what to wear in order to protect your nether regions during a run I would love to know.

February 23rd - LSR of 17 miles today, now I know I can do it!

Been a good week as far as running goes, after last week's golf I got out on the Tuesday for a six miler at the gym, but this time I tried bringing my pace down in preparation for my LSR. Found it quite difficult to maintain a slower pace on the runner as it was very boring, so I did a split run of 35 minutes for the first 3 miles and 25 minutes for the next three which I felt was more beneficial.

I intended doing my LSR on the Thursday, but having booked in to see an osteopath on the Friday I decided to practice my loop I had worked out. I wanted the osteopath to work on my sciatica, so I didn't want to have sore legs at all after a long run.

So off I went at what I wanted to be a minute slower than my normal pace, but although it was productive in terms of working out a route I again ran too fast and need to work on this as I will not last more than 10 miles at that pace. The visit seemed to be quite productive; I had a remedial massage which was essentially a deep tissue massage on my right gluteus and boy was that painful, I didn't know you could push a thumb so hard into a muscle! Anyway, after a half an hour I then had a another massage which was intended to loosen me up for the osteopath, but she also concentrated on the tight muscles in my right leg, mainly around my shin and calf area. Again, this was quite painful and then I had the osteopath come in and bend me in all directions accompanied by some rather alarming clicking noises.

I have another appointment next Friday and though I am not sure about the benefits I can see that a sports massage would be of help and may book one just before the run in April. I ate well over the weekend in terms of good food to fuel my LSR, woke early on Sunday for porridge and then stretched for 20 minutes. The weather was not that good as it was raining a bit and there was quite a gale blowing, but I was ready to go so off I set. I eased into the first lap trying to plod along as easily as I could and although I always find the first mile, mile and a half a problem I was running freely and looking forward to toughing it out. The first six miles went by in just over the hour, which was a bit too fast so I made an effort to slow a bit as I really did want this to be a long slow run. It was quite hard running into the wind sometimes, but you just grit your teeth and push on.

The next six miles were enjoyable as I was plodding along nicely at a slightly slower pace and I completed 12 miles in around two hours and 5 minutes, so not too bad and then the half marathon came up around two hours 16 minutes. By this time I was taking a couple of jelly babies every two miles or so, but no water. There is a reason for this as I had intended to run past my house on each loop and had water waiting for me in the porch, however I have found that I drink far too much and am then busting for a pee, so I had taken it steady and was watching out for any signs that I needed water.

So off on my third loop I went, though I was looking for a maximum of 16 miles as that is what my plan says. I was beginning to feel some niggles, but was spurred on by the thought of running further than I have ever run before AND I had not stopped once which was pleasing. At fifteen and a half miles I was heading home when I noticed my wife in her car alongside me, bless her she was worried as I had been running for nearly three hours and was making sure I was okay! At that stage I had intended to grab some water and then do another two miles, but time was getting on and I still had a lot of things to do so I just added another mile, content that I could have run on and happy with my determination to stay the course.

I finished in two hours and fifty six minutes, not a great time, but as Jim would say, an honest one and it was meant to be a long slow run, which it certainly was. I learnt a lot about fuelling during the run too, I do need some water, but not too much and jelly babies really do work for me, which is good as I find them easy to carry and chew when running.

I ran without stopping for 17 miles and felt reasonably okay, though the ice bath was tough when I got back and my knees have been sore all afternoon. However, that is the furthest I have ever run and I really feel positive about finishing the London Marathon now. That will be my longest training run as I will ease back on the miles. Though my sciatica was okay during the run it is still an issue, as are the knees and hips, so I want to stay in good shape and get to the start line. Pushing myself to run further and faster would probably cause an injury so I am happy to revise my goals and look to finish. I am, after all, running for Cancer Research UK in memory of my brother Neil and the aim has always been to raise money. Happy running everybody, hope the training is going well!

From: Neil Adam
Sent: 26/11/2011 07:50 GMT
To: John Adam
Subject: Charity Event

Hi John,

Here is some news about me, I trust I will be OK for Sat, expect I will. Have arranged for nurses and Carers to come in the afternoon so I can be ready to go out in my black tie! Linda will take me home once I have had enough hope to last the night but with the amount of drugs I am on it will be difficult. That's what will kill me eventually I think. We have 83 people coming on Sat and another lot of donations for the raffle so it should be a good night. We finished off the table settings yesterday, you and Annie are sat next to Linda and I. There will be named place settings, how posh!

Despite the very aggressive nature of his cancer Neil was determined to do something to help improve research into the disease he had and set about raising money for Cancer Research UK. A charity event was organised locally, with Neil as the guest of honour, and along with friends and family we attended an inspirational evening although it was tinged with sadness. The cancer was taking its toll on his body and despite his positive attitude it was a battle he was never going to win. It was obvious that for many of the people who attended this would be the last time they saw Neil alive and that added a certain poignancy to the event.

Despite this it was a wonderful and memorable evening, Neil was a much respected man and it was good for him to be amongst old friends and colleagues.

21 TAPERING AT LAST

March 2nd - 10 miles today, just a short run.

Funny how 10 miles is now a short run and felt like it too, comfortable and easily doable in a good time. After last week's 17 miles I was back on the treadmill on Tuesday after a parent's evening for 3 mile tempo run that turned into 6 miles very easily. If it wasn't for the fact the gym was closing I would have done more which is great after my LSR on the Sunday. Followed that up on Wednesday with a 4 mile run; that made it 100 miles for the month of February which I was very pleased with. Touch wood there have been no issues save for my continued battle with the sciatica, but I had another session on Friday with the osteopath and another sports massage which seemed to have improved things a bit more. I have also booked a 45 min sports massage on the Friday before London to get myself in the best possible shape.

Today I set off into the wind again, so fed up with running in this weather, but it makes you a stronger runner I guess? I meant to run at 10:30 pace like last week, but when I checked I was running at 10 quite comfortably and the last three miles were done at 9:30 pace which is pleasing. I considered running the half marathon distance, but ran out of time as youngest son needed a lift. So, ice bath again which is hell on earth but seems to work and after a while the legs just go numb!

A hot shower and a quick snack before driving him down to meet his friends, I spent the afternoon watching films and relaxing and my legs feel okay. Things are slowly coming together, I checked my hotel booking for Saturday 12th, my wife and I are staying at the Hotel Mercure which is a short walk to the start line at Greenwich Park. Sponsorship is also doing well, now up to £1850 and still much more promised so I should easily meet my target of £2000 which takes the pressure off.

As some of you might be aware I am writing a book about my London Marathon experience called "Running for Neil" and on my training runs I mentally write bits in my head. Today I wrote the introduction as three miles passed by and then rewrote it over the next three miles. I find it very relaxing to let my thoughts wander as I run and it really helped relax me. The book will be dedicated to my brother and I will publish it in one way or another but what started out as a simple story now has another element to factor in, that of the Real Buzz community whose advice and support have kept me going these past 12 months.

So, unlike many of you on here there will be no back story from me, which will be reserved for my book, but suffice to say I will have a lot to say about the incredible community of like-minded individuals who I have never met, but am honoured to call friends. We are now at the business end of training for the various Spring races that are coming up, indeed Reading Half was today, and I wish everybody good luck and great running.

March 8th - There's running in these legs!

It's been a difficult week as after my 10 mile run on Sunday and a feeling of being in control at last I came down with some sort of chest infection on the Monday. This culminated in me losing my voice on the Tuesday, not good for a teacher, and so I was sent home in the afternoon. I didn't feel too bad I just had a really croaky voice and a bit of a dry cough. Anyway, I took the next day off to try and shake it off and then returned to work on Thursday, still croaky, but able to communicate with the pupils and staff in a husky voice, much to their amusement!

Knowing what I do about running with a possible chest infection I cancelled both runs this week and hoped I would be okay by the weekend. The worries start to set in then, you read people's blogs and see how well they are doing and now we at the business end of training etc. Will I lose my fitness in a week, how will I cope on the day now, will my chest clear, all valid but ultimately pointless questions. I was going stir crazy by Saturday morning and was desperate to get out running, but also not wanting to set myself back again. It was a lovely day, perfect for running so I headed to the gym! If there was a problem with my chest I could get in the steam room and try and shift it that way, but as it turned out I ran 6 miles without any problems in less than an hour and felt strong all the way. Legs were fine, knees good, sciatica is much improved and no problems with my chest. Still the odd cough, but I feel confident again and raring to go. I wanted to do a half marathon on the Sunday, but will put that off to next weekend and instead have a light jog. That will be my longest run until the big day as I'm starting to taper, but I am hoping to run more during the week to keep up the fitness.

As you read the blogs you can tell people are getting excited, talk of registration and collecting numbers at Excel, hotels booked, transport organised, Real Buzz picnic planned and an air of expectation and trepidation in equal measure. Details came through today for family members supporting Cancer Research UK runners, so my wife and son will be receiving clappers, cheering sticks, whistles even a loud hailer as well as a Cancer Research UK t-shirt to cheer me on at mile 25. They also get refreshments provided and will meet me later on at CRUK's hospitality area near the finish line. I have ironed on my letters to my running vest, my name 'John' on the front and 'IMO Neil Adam' on the back and it all seems much more real now.

So with just over a month to go what I have learnt in what amounts to 18 months of training, albeit with a gap of 6 months in the middle! Being a sprinter in my youth, quite clearly I am not a long distance runner, but I am stubborn and I am pleased with how I have persevered at an activity which does not come naturally to me.

My body is more capable than I think it is and although I have been careful not to push too hard I am surprised at just how much I can cope with when things get tough. Positive thoughts really help my running and a lot of that comes from the Real Buzz community. Remembering what other people have done or said has really helped my running.

My pace decreases as the distance increases and I seem to have a natural pace which my body settles into as the mileage creeps up. Running is incredibly cathartic and can be quite an emotional activity; I know I am not alone in running through tears at times.

This has been such a great experience, despite the setbacks last year, as the support I had during what were desperate days was incredible and has sustained me and pushed me onto what I expect to be one of the greatest days of my life. I never expected any of this when I signed up to run, it was something I had always wanted to do and when my brother passed away it seemed to be the right time to give it a go.

I joined Real Buzz on a whim, I thought it would be useful to keep a record of my training and maybe get a few tips along the way, I had no expectations of it making much of a difference to the challenge I had set myself. How wrong I was! It has become a huge part of my daily routine and a massive part of my life as I log on quite a few times during the day and really enjoy reading what everybody is doing. It is a place for advice, support, challenges and of course friendship and has been an unexpected bonus in training for the London Marathon.

I am really enjoying the run in to April 13th and look forward to taking part in a great day; hopefully I will get to meet some of the many Real Buzz community? Good running everybody, especially those running tomorrow, good luck!

March 18th - Great run, bad run, good run.....

As always with these things I know not to panic when things go slightly
awry, but this has been an interesting week and I was worried for a while.
Had a couple of great tempo runs during the week, one of which was on a
balmy evening and an absolute joy, ran 5 miles mostly at 9:30 pace with the
last two miles at 9:00 pace and it was the smoothest run I have had for ages.
Things just seemed to flow and I felt great.

So confidence was high leading into Sunday's LSR but for some reason it all
went wrong, though I do know why. Feeling over-confident from the last
run I neglected to stretch properly and fuel properly and it was much
warmer than I am used to. A lesson well learned for April 13th I think, but
as I came round after my first lap of six miles to grab a drink I was feeling
the heat and by then it was a bit too late though at the time I didn't
recognise it. Half way round the second lap I began to struggle a bit and
this altered my running style so much so that I began to feel pain in my left
knee. Shrugging this off as just a niggle I ran on, but then common sense
got the better of me and I decided to finish after only two laps.

By this time my knee was very sore on the outside which I found quite
worrying. I got into the ice bath and soaked for 20 minutes then iced the
knee for another 30 minutes before walking gently around the house. From
the soreness it felt like the dreaded IT band injury and I began to worry
even more. Resting for most of the day I had a good night's sleep and woke
up wondering how the knee would react. It seemed okay, not in any way
like the symptoms of an IT band injury, but I was cautious and took it
steady throughout the day.

Of course I got back at the end of the day to my magazine giving me all the
details I need for registering etc. which only served to panic me even more!
Common sense prevailed, it was just a strain caused by running badly which
in turn had been caused by poor preparation, but I wanted to test out the
knee as soon as I could. So today I headed to the gym and after stretching
carefully I set the runner for three miles with a slow walking warm up first.
I Hour later of running within myself and not a twinge from the knee I am
a happy man and everything is back on track. The run felt pleasantly
comfortable, short and easy which is how I want to run on the day, but I
must be mindful of the conditions and fuel sensibly as well as take on fluids
before I need them, particularly if it is a warm day.

So now I am even more excited than I was before, though probably
because I was quite worried for a while. I have read the magazine from

cover to cover and twice more, looked at the map and visualised where I might be and at what times and I just cannot imagine what the day will be like, but I know it will be a wonderful experience.

As I do not want to get an injury so close to the day. I will do one more LSR, but at the gym to make sure I am consistent in my style and I get the miles under my belt. I know I can run 17 miles when I have done everything right, but I would like to get another three hour run in before the day itself, just for peace of mind. I will also switch my shorter tempo runs to the road during the week, but practise taking on fluids as well as trying out the Lucozade Sport drink to see how that affects me.

I have also finally reached my target weight of 13 stone, the less I have to cart around 26 mile 385 yards the better as I was 14 ½ stone at Christmas despite training for three months previously so I am pleased with that. It's carbohydrates for me now as I don't want to lose any more weight, but I do feel much better for it. I feel I have done the best I can, given my various issues, and I am feeling much more confident, especially after tonight's run.

Good running everybody and for those running London, not long to go now!

March 23rd - Half Marathon completed, time to taper now!

As most of you know, my injury issues have forced me to adopt a rather different plan to last year, but I feel it has worked for me and today I wanted to get a half marathon under my belt before the big day. I know many of you are attempting 18 and 20 milers, but I have to be realistic and want to get to the start line as healthy as I can be. My last long run was 17 miles three weeks ago and I wanted to get another long run in last week, but had some issues with my knee. So this week I have run a 6 miles and 3 miles in preparation for 13.1 today. My knee was a bit sore on Friday in a different place, so I was a bit worried, but it does not stop me running at all, just a niggle that I am aware of.

Today I did everything that I will do on the big day, got up early and had a big bowl of porridge, a banana and drank some water after a cup of tea. Then I got my kit ready, including my water and and took it easy whilst sorting out some music to run to. Finally I started to stretch carefully as well as strapping the knee mostly as a precaution. I set off steadily and the first 3 miles were not as good as I would have hoped which I put down to rather too much porridge, even though that was now two and half hours ago! Anyway, the next 3 were an improvement and I have found that working in batches of 3 works for me as that is what I am used to. After another mile though I was busting for the toilet so popped behind a tree and then set off again, 7 in the bank and feeling okay. All this time I was also taking a jelly baby every mile and this also seemed to work ok. I got to 10 miles in a reasonable time; I wasn't pushing it all and was trying to run within myself as well as little slower than I would normally.

Finally I put on a little burst over the last mile feeling reasonably okay and finished the half marathon, or 13.1 miles in just under 2 hours 15 minutes at an average pace of 10.18 which was a bit faster than I wanted, but I'm not complaining as I got it done, didn't crash and burn and after a cold bath, hot shower and something to eat I feel okay.

So, I'm tapering now and will run 3 miles on Tuesday and another on Friday followed by 9 miles on Sunday and then cutback to 6 miles next Sunday ready for the last week of rest. It is so close now I am a bag of nerves and excited at the same time. I know I can do it, but I really want to enjoy the day and I hope that the weather is going to be okay. As I finished today it started to hail and then 10 minutes later it was sunny, hope it doesn't do that on the day!

Everybody has been doing some great runs and it seems that people are more than ready for the various challenges ahead. We are all running for very personal reasons and it has been fantastic to be part of the Real Buzz community. Looking forward to hopefully meeting a few in London, less than three weeks to go!

March 29th - Nervous, but feeling positive.

Just over two weeks to go now and there is no doubt I am feeling very nervous, yet incredibly excited about the run on the 13th. Since last Sunday's half marathon I have eased back a bit though I did play netball for the staff against the school's first team on Tuesday! They were very good, but having played National League Basketball in my youth I played goal shooter, managed to score quite a lot very easily and we won. My colleagues were worried about me getting injured, but I took it easy and then afterwards went to the gym for a 3 mile run.

I actually ached the next day as I had been using muscles I was not used to using and so took a few days off before my next run, but then my knee started to trouble me again, nothing serious, just a bit of soreness and so I dropped my run on Friday and bought forward my 8 mile run from Sunday to today. What a lovely day to run as well, the sun was shining but it was not too hot so I had a bagel and a banana early for breakfast before getting myself kitted out and stretching well before setting off with some jelly babies.

As I sweat quite a lot from my forehead I thought I would try a thin baseball cap and sunglasses which worked well, so I will wear those on the day. The run was nice and steady and I settled into a gentle plod along familiar roads aware of the fact that this would be my last longish run even though I was thinking of it as a short run...... 8 miles...... short......, who would have thought I would ever have thought of an 8 mile run as a short run!

Anyway the miles ticked off nicely and my thoughts began to wander as I began to imagine the crowds and the noise. I have got so used to running on my own, lost in my thoughts that I find it difficult to comprehend just what the day will be like, but I know it will be one amazing day. I felt comfortable at the pace I was running at and have pretty much decided that I will try to seek out the 4:30 pace runner and see how I go. I got back expecting to see a pace time of 10.30 miles as I was running quite slow only to find that I was running 10 minute miles pretty consistently for the whole of the run which was pleasing.

My mind set as I finish is one of knowing that I can keep that pace going and so I stopped and walked another half mile to ease back and then it was time for my last ice bath. I hate them, but they do work and after 5 minutes everything goes numb anyway, it's just getting in that is tough. After that I had a warm bath and felt okay, knees were both fine, sciatica I manage and have got used to, as much as you can get used to sciatica, and I feel more positive than ever. I know it is not going to be easy, but as many people have said, if it were easy everybody would do it.

I am now on holiday for three weeks, so ideal preparation for the big day, so, a couple of easy runs next week, followed by one more last run the week after and I am ready for the race of my life. I have decided that to try and fit everything in on the Saturday would be crazy, so I will head up to Excel on either the Wednesday or the Thursday and spend a reasonable amount of time looking around and soaking up the atmosphere. Then on Saturday my wife and I can head to my brother-in-laws and drop our youngest son off as we have a hotel booked near the start line, but on the way we can make a detour to Hyde Park.

There are a few things I need to sort out before the day, but I have settled on suitable nutrition, my water intake, what I will wear and a pace that is comfortable. I have done the training, put in the hard miles and feel incredibly proud of myself for not giving up when it would have been so easy to do so. I also never forget that I am 'Running for Neil' and have raised over £2300 so far for Cancer Research UK and the donations are still coming in.

From: Neil Adam
Sent: 15/12/2011 12:48 GMT
To: John Adam
Subject: Christmas wishes

Hi John
Looking forward to seeing you on Christmas day, the fountain is great and I have briefed the landscaper to add some more plants and trees in the New Year, will tell you about it. My tree present is also here. a planting ceremony was on Saturday in lovely sunshine. I think Christmas Eve will be OK and mild. The new house is fantastic for me, with lots of space inside and out to go with my wheelchair. And the views are great, especially from the lounge, where my bed is now. The house is also very warm and snug and more so with the wood burning stove alight. My health seems to be stable at the moment thanks to drugs and I think I have a good chance of seeing Easter and the bulbs coming through in the garden, who knows with the tumour in my head? Have a good Christmas and just count your blessings like I still do every day despite my situation.

So Christmas came around and Neil was in excellent spirits mentally, though his body had taken quite a battering. The tumour was now in his head and had affected his face causing the left side to droop, but he remained positive and had set himself a new target of Easter. He was enjoying the house a lot which was wonderful as it had been his driving force throughout the last two years. He was able to move around on his wheelchair and take in the views of the valley and he very much enjoyed researching, buying and adding various garden features. These gave him an enormous amount of pleasure and that was strangely comforting.

Given everything he had gone through, throughout all his trials and tribulations, all the pain and the discomfort, his parting words to me were 'count your blessings' something our mum used to say. That serves as a comfort to me, our mother lived through him and in turn he lives though me. I have some wonderful memories of a truly remarkable brother, one who fought his cancer with a determination to live that was an inspiration to all those who knew him.

22 ONE EYE ON THE PRIZE

April 5th - Getting ready and a last road run before VLM.

It's been an interesting week as I've been on holiday and the rest of the family haven't. Each day has started with thoughts of how I might pass the hours, yet all of sudden it is 5.00pm, the best part of the day has gone and I don't appear to have achieved anything worthwhile!

With a couple of easy 3 milers at the gym, some visits to the sports departments of various malls and quite a few walks with the dog, the days have just flown by and here we are with just seven days to go. I have been very careful with everything I have done, whether it was running, walking, driving or just basic chores just in case something happens to me, stupid I know, but it is so close now.

Hollywood posted a message to me to look back at my first ever post on here back in October 2012 and reflect on just how far I have come. He's right of course; it has been an incredible journey, 18 months of training, injuries, an operation and recovery with emotions laid bare and inspirational messages of support throughout. I have learnt a lot about myself along the way, but I have also learnt a lot about others on here, people who I have yet to meet. The support, the advice, the commitment and the passion have been the driving force behind me getting to this point and now the prize is not far away.

These last few days I have been attending to the small details so that I don't have to worry too much next weekend and particularly Sunday. So I ordered some more compression socks as the others were past their best and also some running shorts. My kit is now complete and I know that I will be comfortable running in it all as long as I have prepared as I usually do. The new trainers have been brilliant, so comfortable so I'm hoping they will not cause any issues in the latter stages of the race.

I have also started editing the first draft of my book and looking back through my brother's emails to me during his illness. They have not been easy to read and I confess they moved me to tears on a number of occasions, but as I read through them I realised that there was always hope in every single one of them. He never gave up, never gave in and fought so bravely to the bitter end and I will take that with me next Sunday.

So today I ran 5 miles as my last short long run and I ran it with my wife as she wanted to run with me. We went out in matching yellow hi-viz tops as it was raining a bit, but it was a lovely run, despite getting soaked, as I don't usually run with anybody. Bought it home to me how much easier it is running with someone so goodness knows what it will feel like next Sunday.

So two more runs at the gym and then a visit to the Expo at Excel to register and get my timing chip and number. I am really looking forward to that and also hoping to meet a few more of the Real Buzz community for the first time. Good luck to those of you running tomorrow J

April 10th A life changing experience.

As the weekend nears I have managed a couple of gentle runs at the gym and the next time I lace on my trainers will be before the start of the London Marathon. The week started on Sunday tracking various runners in Paris and Brighton and how exhausting was that as the miles ticked by the excitement built as mentally you tried to imagine what each one of them was going through. The blogs this week have revealed some incredible stories of courage in the face of adversity, but in true Real Buzz spirit they all made it home and congratulations to every one of you, an amazing achievement. The thing is, unless you are a runner no one really understands the challenge each one of us faces and what it takes to complete a marathon, but the Real Buzz community appreciate what an undertaking it is and that is why there was such support on Sunday, support for people I have not even met and who will, in turn, support me on Sunday.

Today I went to the Virgin Marathon Expo at the Excel in London to register and after a long journey via Victoria I made it to the exhibition by 12:00. Before too long I had got my number and timing chip, which made it seem even more real, and then wandered into a runner's dream scenario. If you weren't a runner before you sure as hell should be walking round that exhibition. I made it to the coffee area and watched an Interview with Stephen Kiprotich, Olympic and World marathon champion. He was interesting to listen to and also quite small in stature, he looks bigger on the TV!

Anyway, I managed to catch up with Jim, Sacha, Dave, Jane and Keith, who I only knew from their Real Buzz blogs, but who had been a tremendous source of inspiration during my training. It was wonderful to meet them at last and I am looking forward to meeting the rest of the Real Buzz community on Saturday the day before the run. I had a great time talking about various injuries, training runs and orange hot pants before having a last look around. It was really nice to meet up today and put me at ease a bit as I know I'm not alone in my feelings about the day.

The Expo was just brilliant and really got me in the mood to run, as if I wasn't excited enough already. Then it was home to reflect on the day and tomorrow I am getting everything packed and ready before heading to London on Saturday. I have a hotel booked near Greenwich Park, a short walk to the red start and a table booked at a local Italian restaurant for some pre-run pasta, though not too much!

So this is the last post before the run on Sunday and what a journey it has been so far! Many miles of training in the cold, wet, dark days of winter are now behind me. The injuries, the aches and pains and, in my case, a small operation. All done now and I am ready for the challenge of my life and that is somewhat of an alien prospect for me. I have never been more focussed in my life, the London Marathon has been my every waking thought since I decided to run and that is relatively unusual for me. In contrast to my brother Neil I have generally taken the easy path, whereas he was driven to do well in life, my mantra has been, like my mother, 'what will be will be', I have never forced an issue, never really pushed the boundaries. Over the course of the last eighteen months I have had to ask quite a few questions of myself. As you get older you do tend to look back and wonder, what if? Training for the London Marathon has made me question much of my life to date and I thought it useful to write down my back story as I try to make sense of who I am, or indeed, who I was?

I was the sporty one in the family, although I was clearly not stupid, Neil was the academic and I played sport, a lot of sport. I was a very good high jumper from an early age and was county champion every year throughout my secondary years, even going to the All England Schools Championships in 1973 at Bebbington. Also there were a couple of little known athletes, Sebastian Coe and Steve Ovett, both of whom won their events easily, surprisingly. They were rising stars, though little did I know that at the time. Me, I never made it past the qualifying stage, natural talent could only take me so far, but I was never dedicated enough to train seriously. I often wonder what I might have achieved had I been bothered to work at it as I became county champion again two years later when I was eighteen having switched from straddle to the 'Fosbury Flop', but I attended my brother's wedding instead and never really jumped much again, a shame as I was clearing nearly six foot at the time.

By this time though, basketball had taken over my life, despite being quite a good rugby player, on the wing as you ask, I grew quite tall and my PE teacher called me into the gym when I was 14, quite a late introduction, but

I really enjoyed it and loved everything about the game. I became a proficient shooter, especially the jump shot and in particular a 'Three Pointer' and played as a forward; despite being tall I was quick on court and pretty soon I was playing at county level. Again, I was not driven enough to take it even further and never got the chance to move higher.

As I played a lot of sport I did not really work as hard as I could on my studies but, I got on well with my physical education teachers, indeed, by the age of fifteen I was playing in the local men's leagues with them and they gave me the idea of applying to PE college. At that time there were a number of very good specialist colleges and I chose St Paul's in Cheltenham. Half way through the first term of the lower Sixth I was awarded an unconditional place and pretty much stopped working too hard, instead enjoying my last year and a half of the sixth form. I had inherited my brother's scooter and had a great social life to keep me occupied when I wasn't playing basketball.

Three years in Cheltenham where I had the time of my life, from being a big fish in small pond I found myself surrounded by international sportsmen from all walks of life. It was a big wake up call, but I will always fondly remember my time at St Paul's, it was the mid-70s and the disco era was in full swing though punk was just around the corner, interesting times. Teaching practice was a bit of a shock, suddenly I was expected to take charge of a bunch of children I had never met before and suddenly life got serious. I coped, but it wasn't until I got my first job in Portsmouth that I really began to learn how to handle the lesser motivated child.

I was fortunate that about that time basketball was starting to become much bigger in the UK and was even televised by Channel 4 at one stage. I joined the local team and was also selected to play for the solent area team. After a short trial with Solent Stars, I eventually got my chance to play National League Basketball for Portsmouth, but for only one season unfortunately. However, it was an enjoyable season, I learnt a lot playing with some very good American players, but ultimately it was another case of, if only I had taken it more seriously when I was younger. Natural talent can get you so far, but you need to be dedicated to go further and I just did not have the drive that my brother had.

I didn't go into teaching to make money, it seemed like a great way to keep doing the things I liked to do and the holidays were great, but over the years I have really learnt to love my job, working with children has been a wonderful career and I have taught some lovely people over the years, some of whom are still in touch with me today. Physical Education was not the career for me however and I have retrained a couple of times and have taught Computing for the last twenty years. I seemed to have an aptitude for using, fixing or configuring computers and have found it a fascinating subject to teach, but again, this was another case of, what if? Many people have asked me, as I've fixed their PC or Laptop, why don't you leave teaching there are plenty of jobs in the computer industry, you could earn more money? The answer is, I like what I do, I'm quite good at what I do and it gives me a good quality of life. I'll never be rich, but I'll be happy and that's something you can't put a price on, again, my mother's influence coming through.

So when Sunday arrives and I find myself standing amongst upwards of 36,000 people, what have I learnt from this experience? I am not my brother and if I had had the drive he had would I have achieved more in my life, would I have been happier, richer, I will never know. However, the last eighteen months have changed me in many ways and I know that when I line up on Sunday, although I can look back on plenty of missed opportunities and numerous mistakes, I am not a quitter and I will conquer one of the greatest challenges of my life; if there is one thing I have learnt from this whole experience it is that life is there to be lived and adversity is what makes us who we are. Good luck on Sunday everybody, see you on the other side!

April 13th - I am a Marathon Runner

Well I did it, not in quite the way I envisaged I would, but I did it, I got round the course and I got my medal; no one can take that away from me. More importantly I ran for my brother and for Cancer Research UK and to date I have raised almost £3500 which I'm very pleased with.

So how did the weekend go? Well despite initial feelings of disappointment, after a period of reflection and some lovely messages of support from Real Buzzers and family and friends I would say that it has to rank up there as one of the most amazing experiences of my life.

I travelled up to London with my extremely supportive wife who has been an absolute rock during the last 18 months. We left the car at Balham whilst she spent some time with her family and I travelled to the Real Buzz picnic at Hyde Park. That was such an enjoyable afternoon spent with people I had not met before apart from a few at the Expo on the Thursday. What a really lovely bunch of people who all had a common goal and a purpose and who had been so supportive in my efforts to get to the start line.

After that I headed back to the centre of London to meet my wife and we made our way to the Hotel in Greenwich which would allow me a short walk to the start line in the morning. We had a meal at a restaurant by the Cutty Sark overlooking the Thames, pasta obviously, and generally relaxed and soaked up the atmosphere. The barriers were up, but it was hard to believe I would be running around there the next day.

A fairly sleepless night followed whilst I mulled over the enormity of the challenge and went through all the details again and again. An early breakfast was followed by the preparation, vaseline, compression socks, timing chip, number, bum bag, jelly babies, phone, Cancer Research UK bin liner and a drink every few minutes followed by a visit to the toilet every few minutes. It was all done and checked by 8:30 and we walked up to the start. I was not prepared for what greeted me, thousands of runners all decked out in a multitude of colour and fancy dress, an unbelievable sight.

My wife had to leave me then which was an emotional parting of course, she has been behind me the whole way and I can't thank her enough. So, on my own now I made my way to the baggage lorries which were incredibly efficient. Then I needed the toilet again obviously and so did everybody else, amazing queues snaking around the area. Soon we were called to the start and there followed some tense moments before we started to move and then suddenly I was running. Somehow I found myself running near the 4:15 pacer which was rather silly so I eased back and then suddenly I was caught by Vin, Dave (DCW), Jane and Lorna and was privileged to run with a team of Real Buzzers for some eight miles before I started to have a few issues with my knee unfortunately.

Of all the problems I expected it was not my knee which had not given me any problems in training up to that point, but I started to feel a niggling pain at the site of the operation so I slowed a bit to see how it would react. At Tower Bridge which I reached in around 2:20 I felt okay, but I stopped for a picture and then found it hard to pick up the pace as my knee was now very sore.

I walked just after the Bridge, but savoured the moments before as it was a most spectacular sight, an amazing amount of people all shouting, screaming even, support and encouragement. I found the support got me round as I decided to adopt a run/walk strategy as I was determined to finish, for Neil, for all the very generous people who had donated and for the Real Buzzers who had supported me.

So, I toughed it out, jogging when I could and walking when I had to and though I was gutted to be walking at times, I knew it was a necessity if I were to get round. Those who were tracking knew there was an issue as I slowed at 25K and were a little concerned, but mile by mile I pushed on, the encouragement was incredible, I will always remember the words of support (though it has to be said that many people are called John in London, so it wasn't always for me!) as well as the noise which was mind-blowing, particularly around Canary Wharf!

As I jogged along the Embankment grimacing in pain I heard my lovely wife shouting and ran over for a hug and to explain the problem which gave me the energy for the final push to the end. I shall never forget the feeling of turning into the Mall and seeing that finish line. I had envisaged tears of emotion, but it was one of relief as I ran over the line to get my medal. 5:25 I think, not brilliant, an hour slower than my targeted time, but only 25 min slower than my expected time.

After a quick visit to the medical facility to ice my knee I met up with my wife and we went to the reception at Cancer Research UK for some much need sustenance. My wife chided me for being negative as I was I bit down about how it had gone and she was right. Messages of congratulations came in thick and fast and from everybody and very soon I was indeed feeling proud of myself.

For my brother Neil, I miss you every day and think of you often, if you are looking down I ran it for you, I am a Marathon Runner.

There were no more emails from my brother as his health deteriorated rapidly and apart from a short text on New Year's Eve, communication ceased. The next paragraph is taken from my Just Giving page which was set up after I gained my place in the London Marathon.

'Neil sadly passed away on 21st January 2012 after a long and very brave battle. He displayed an amazing spirit throughout his illness which he fought with absolute dignity. He was determined to do as much as he could in the time that he had and with the help of friends and family, set about raising funds for Cancer Research UK. I am running the London Marathon in April of this year, in honour of my brother and would appreciate your support in doing so. All money donated will go towards beating this terrible disease'.

I have been amazed at the generosity of people and at the time of publication the total stands at an incredible £3519.20.

23 EPILOGUE

It's a week since I completed the London Marathon, time enough for me to reflect on the weekend and look back on what was arguably one of the most amazing experiences of my life. What started as a simple pledge to raise money turned into a life-changing event. Training to run a marathon is not easy and takes a certain amount of discipline, something that I am not normally very good at. Actually running the marathon is not just a physical exercise either, it also requires a degree of mental strength, again, something that is not one of my strong points.

It wasn't until the letter from Cancer Research UK arrived in October confirming my place that it became a reality and although there was a certain measure of bravado in my commitment to run for a charity I fully intended to honour that commitment. However, it was clear to me that I had seriously underestimated just how much of a challenge it would be. 26.2 miles is an awfully long way at any age, but I was now 55 and suffering various issues due to the sports I had played in my youth, my knees in particular.

The enormity of the challenge was not as overtly obvious to me in the early stages and certainly I trained way too hard too quickly. This resulted in me injuring myself and having to defer, though there is no doubt that I benefitted from the injury in the long run. It gave me a respect for the distance and respect for the people who run marathons. It also had added benefits in the form of new friends from the Real Buzz community, people from all walks of life running for many different reasons, some heart-breaking but never less than inspirational. The support and advice I was given from these people can never be under-estimated and I will be forever grateful to them all.

Having not met any of them until a few days before the London Marathon I am honoured to call them my friends. They were instrumental in getting me to the start line, after my deferral I was unsure if I would ever be able to make good my promise to my brother, but they never gave up on me and encouraged me all the way. During my training they were a constant source of advice and support and even during the run itself there was a Real Buzz presence that drove me on towards the finish line.

The long hours of training, the various injuries, the knee operation and recovery, obtaining the right kit, organising nutrition and making sure I did not become dehydrated; running became my obsession, it consumed my every waking thought. If I wasn't thinking about the last training run I was thinking about the next training run. Slowly I began to believe that I could do it, as the runs became longer and longer I realised that I was becoming mentally stronger and much more determined. Although I was running slower due to the various issues I had, I was running well and that gave me confidence. For me it was never about time, it was about finishing although I wanted to do myself justice.

It was the early hills that caused the problem with my knee, something that I had not anticipated and crucially, something I had not trained for. Despite being unable to run as much as I would have wanted to I made it to the end and achieved what I had set out to do, to run the London Marathon and to raise as much money as possible for Cancer Research UK. I'm not ashamed to say I wore my finishers' shirt and medal that evening and the messages of congratulations were overwhelming, so much so that my initial disappointment very soon became a feeling of pride.

Committing myself to run the London Marathon and raise funds has been the biggest challenge of my life and probably one of the most selfless acts I have ever done. For once it wasn't about me and it wasn't for me and that has changed me, I hope, for the better. I have learnt a lot about myself as well, running alone gives you time to think and I have certainly reflected on who I am. I am certainly proud of my achievement, not many people ever run the distance and the experience was unforgettable. It is a weekend that I will remember with affection for the rest of my life irrespective of the time it took to run, I am and always will be a marathon runner and I know that Neil would have been amongst the first to congratulate me.

ABOUT THE AUTHOR

John Adam has been in education for some thirty six years, although he has taught a variety of subjects. Having left St Paul's College Cheltenham with a Cert Ed in 1978 he went onto teach Physical Education for some years before retraining in Technology at King Alfred's College in Winchester.

He later graduated from King's College, London gaining an M.A.Ed. in Computers in Education, and has taught Computing for the last twenty five years at various educational establishments.

Printed in Great Britain
by Amazon.co.uk, Ltd.,
Marston Gate.